Living Thankfully

PUBLISHED FOR THE DEAN AND CHAPTER
OF THE CATHEDRAL CHURCH OF ST. JOHN THE DIVINE

A CATHEDRAL BOOK

THE CONTRIBUTORS 🐦

THE REVEREND THOMAS VAN B. BARRETT, D.D., the Rector of St. John's Church, Tallahassee, Florida, was formerly the Executive Secretary of the Division of College Work.

MRS. DORA P. CHAPLIN, S.T.D., is Assistant Professor of Pastoral Theology at the General Theological Seminary, New York City, and was formerly Associate Secretary in the Division of Leadership Training, Department of Christian Education, The National Council.

THE VERY REVEREND JOHN B. COBURN, D.D., is Dean and Professor of Pastoral Theology at the Episcopal Theological School, Cambridge, Massachusetts, and was Chaplain of Amherst College, and Dean of Trinity Cathedral, Newark, New Jersey.

THE REVEREND LESLIE J. A. LANG is the Rector of St. Peter's Church in Westchester, a Trustee of the Cathedral Church of St. John the Divine, and formerly was Rector of St. Edward the Martyr, New York City.

THE REVEREND JOHN ELLIS LARGE, D.D., formerly Rector of the Church of the Heavenly Rest, New York City, now is Rector of St. Boniface's Church, Sarasota, Florida.

THE REVEREND CYRIL C. RICHARDSON, TH.D., is Washburn Professor of Church History, and Director of Graduate Studies at Union Theological Seminary, New York City.

THE REVEREND EDWARD N. WEST, TH.D., LITT.D., has been the Canon Sacrist of the Cathedral Church of St. John the Divine, New York City, for the past twenty years; and Lecturer in Liturgics at the General Theological Seminary, New York City.

THE REVEREND SAMUEL J. WYLIE, S.T.M., is the Rector of the Church of the Advent, Boston, Massachusetts, and was formerly the Associate Secretary, Division of College Work, The National Council.

Living Thankfully

THE CHRISTIAN AND THE SACRAMENTS

& *edited by* *HAROLD R. LANDON*

GREENWICH · CONNECTICUT · 1961

ACKNOWLEDGMENT

Grateful acknowledgment is made for permission to use the following:

To Brandt & Brandt, Agent—Stephen Vincent Benet, "A Child Is Born," from *We Stand United and Other Radio Scripts* (Holt, Rinehart & Winston, Inc.). Copyright 1942 by Stephen Vincent Benet.

To Annie Laurie Williams, Agent—Alan Paton, "Meditation, For a Young Boy Confirmed." Copyright 1954 by Alan Paton.

Preface ॐ

Living Thankfully has grown out of papers given at the School of Worship of the Diocese of New York. It combines the papers given in three successive years. The book was not originally planned as a whole, but will nevertheless be found to have a remarkable unity and coherence. This is not by accident.

The four papers on the Holy Communion constitute the original core of the book and were given at the 1958 School of Worship under the general title of "God's Holy Communion with His People."

When planning the lectures for the following year, it was decided by the Cathedral Chapter, and by the Episcopal Churchwomen, who jointly sponsor the School, to go on to a consideration of Baptism and Confirmation as the foundation of the sacramental life. The theme of the 1959 School became, accordingly, "Living Eucharistically" and included the lectures on Baptism, Preparing for the Sacramental Life, Confirmation, and Living Eucharistically. Our purpose then was to publish the eight lectures under the title *Living Thankfully.*

However, before the conclusion of these lectures, it became apparent to the Dean and Chapter that a more valuable book would be obtained by treating the remaining sacramental rites of the Church in a third series of lectures. Thus, the 1960 School dealt with these under the general theme—taken from the Venite—"In His Hand."

As a result, we are able to present a single book dealing with all the sacraments. Such books are all too few, and this book has the practical advantage of having been prepared for lay people. Moreover, nothing has been sacrificed in the way of scholarly understanding and perception.

The reception of these papers originally was most enthusiastic, and the demand for their publication has been clamorous.

The Dean and Chapter are happy to present within the covers of a single book a scholarly and profound treatment of the Sacraments of the Church which we believe will be in wide demand not only for Confirmation classes and study groups, but by all seeking a deeper understanding of the sacramental life of the Church.

The three main divisions of the book preserve the themes of the three successive Schools of Worship. The editor's introduction provides a summary of the central theme of the book: Through the sacramental life of the Church we come to behold *God's gracious hand* in all his works. And in the final chapter we are brought to what is the end and aim of the sacramental life—*Living Thankfully.*

THE EDITOR

Contents 🙾

PREFACE — v

INTRODUCTION — 3

I. The Preparation for Sacramental Living

ONE — HOLY BAPTISM — 13
SAMUEL J. WYLIE

TWO — PREPARING FOR THE SACRAMENTAL LIFE — 28
DORA P. CHAPLIN

THREE — CONFIRMATION — 45
EDWARD N. WEST

II. God's Holy Communion with His People

FOUR — THE HEAVENLY BANQUET — 67
CYRIL C. RICHARDSON

FIVE — THE KNOWLEDGE OF THE RISEN LORD — 75
EDWARD N. WEST

vii

Six   THE HOLY SACRIFICE   91
         Cyril C. Richardson

Seven   THE COMMUNION   99
         Edward N. West

III. In His Hand

Eight   THE ASSURING HAND: ABSOLUTION   121
         Leslie J. A. Lang

Nine   THE HEALING HAND: UNCTION   132
         John Ellis Large

Ten   JOINING HANDS: HOLY MATRIMONY   148
         Thomas Van B. Barrett

Eleven   APOSTOLIC HANDS: HOLY ORDER   170
         Edward N. West

IV. The Life of Thankfulness

Twelve   LIVING EUCHARISTICALLY   195
         John B. Coburn

Notes   211

Living Thankfully

Introduction ह✤

*Open, we pray thee, our eyes to behold
thy gracious hand in all thy works.*

The great mystery upon which the Christian Church is founded is the mystery of the sacramental presence of our Lord. After his death, Christ manifested himself to the disciples in the breaking of bread. Thus he made known to them that he was risen from the dead and is alive forevermore, and this he continues to make known wherever his disciples gather and break bread together. The Church lives in the power of his resurrection—a power which is renewed in every believer's heart whenever he receives by faith the blessed sacrament of the Body and Blood of Christ.

Through the Holy Supper an altogether new principle has entered into life—the *sacramental principle*. Or rather, not a new principle, for sacraments are as old as life itself, but the establishment of this principle in a new and powerful way.

The principle of sacraments is this: that the material

is made the instrument, the servant, of the spiritual. The simple, ordinary things of everyday life are seen and felt to be charged with eternal meaning and are made the vehicle through which the power of the eternal enters into life.

What is more common, what is more a part of everyday life than eating, the breaking of bread? But through the Holy Supper this necessary part of the daily routine is made the means through which God imparts himself in a most wonderful way. This common act of everyday becomes the means through which Christ is imparted to the world. He manifests himself to his disciples in the breaking of bread. Thus God is seen to shine through the common, ordinary things of life.

Christ has given to the world a new principle through which we see life itself as a sacrament: all life is a means through which God imparts himself. Every bush is aflame with God, and therefore we are enjoined like Moses to "put off thy shoes from off thy feet, for the place whereon thou standest is holy ground." In the light of this sublime fact, we are led to pray in the words of the Prayer Book, "Open, we pray thee, our eyes to behold thy *gracious hand* in all thy works."

I

Consider, then, first of all, the universe itself is a sacrament, the outward sign of an inward meaning. When one beholds the universe in its totality, one is beset with an indescribable sense of awe and mystery. It was not made to man's measurements, or on a scale man can conceive. And yet, when one beholds the sun and moon and stars, each moving in its established order and orbit—the stars are always on time—one is led to declare with the psalmist, "The heavens declare the glory of God; and the firmament showeth his handywork."

Consider some of the smallest things in nature! For example, snowflakes, each with an infinite complexity of design and no two exactly alike. Surely one is driven to say: There must be a Designer—an intelligence beyond our ability to grasp—who has designed this created world. The creation posits a Creator. The childlike mind understands this; the sophisticated mind sometimes forgets it. If an archaeologist digging in ancient ruins discovers a crude cutting tool like an ax or a knife, he will tell you something of the prehistoric man who fashioned it. Likewise we, as rational beings, are driven again and again to the logic that back of this created world is a Creator, a highly creative Mind, infinitely greater than the human mind can conceive.

Again, consider the lilies how they grow! The Creator is an artist as every human being knows who has ever seen the sun go down in a blaze of glory, or beheld the pure beauty of flowers on the mountainside, or the hills aflame on an autumn day.

Jesus found signs of God everywhere in nature, signs both of his providence and of his mercy. "Behold the fowls of the air: for they sow not, neither do they reap, nor gather into barns; yet your heavenly Father feedeth them. Are ye not much better than they?" "God openest his hand and fillest all things living with plenteousness." That is the miracle of life on the earth—the miracle which is made new every springtime when the sap rises in the trees and the flowers bud, the miracle by which the face of the earth is renewed and man is given the promise of his sustenance on the earth: "While the earth remaineth, seedtime and harvest, and cold and heat, and summer and winter, and day and night shall not cease."

Moreover, God's is a merciful providence. "He maketh his sun to rise on the evil and the good, and sendeth rain on the just and on the unjust." Such benevolence on the part of the Almighty is beyond the power of man to conceive—man, who is bent on destroying his enemies. He, by whom are all things, and in whom are all things, is "long suffering, slow to anger, plenteous in mercy." Of this we are reminded by every sunrise and every shower. The created world is a sign and a promise of him who made it. God has left his footprints on the sands of time. The universe is a sacrament!

II

Consider also that man's life on earth is a sacrament. "The spirit of man is the candle of the Lord." The living, questing, perceiving, inquiring, unresting spirit of man made in the image of God is the best clue we have of our Maker. Through the nature and being of man we read the nature and being of God. The psalmist writes: "What is man that thou art mindful of him, or the Son of Man that thou visitest him?" What indeed?

And yet, man, in the highest reaches of his spirit as philosopher, as scientist, as artist, or saint, is the best indicator of God. That is the meaning of the Incarnation: the highest and most perfect representative of man is at the same time the revelation of God. "He that has seen me has seen the Father." Speaking of the Incarnation, St. John writes in the prologue to his Gospel: "And the Word was made flesh, and dwelt among us (and we beheld his glory, the glory as of the only begotten of the Father), full of grace and truth." The life, death, and resurrection of our Lord is a sacrament through which we perceive not only the nature of man but also the nature of God. In him the inner meaning of our life is disclosed.

The best part of man's life is surely not the material constructs of his life: his tools, his houses, his buildings, his machines, although even these are an expression of the nature of man as architect, builder, manufacturer. The best part of man's life is the spiritual: his thoughts, his memory, his feeling, his imagination, and his affections. The best part of man's life is that part which is not visible. Man is spirit. The outward forms of man's life are an expression of his spirit, which is to say, they are sacraments. Take words as an example. A scientist can give you an exact description of how sound is produced and can measure its wave length, intensity, and pitch. No scientist as scientist, however, can tell you the beauty of words, their power and significance in man's life—a mother's lullaby, a lover's promise, Ruth's promise of loyalty to her mother-in-law, "For whither thou goest, I will go . . . the Lord do so to me, and more also, if ought but death part me and thee"—words which are echoed in the marriage service. Or hear David's lament over his son: "O my son Absalom, my son, my son, Absalom! Would God I had died for thee, O Absalom, my son, my son!" What power there is in words!

Everywhere we find that man's life is made up of sacraments: What is a book but the outward expression of the workings of the mind? A painting but the outward expression of the soul of an artist? The handclasp but the outward expression of the bond of friendship? Buildings and monuments are sacraments. The pyramids are living symbols of the question as old as man: "If a man die, shall he live again?" Banks, with their massive stones and solid columns, are expressions of man's faith in the integrity of his fellowmen, a faith which is grounded in the structure of the universe. Or a church with its spires and flying buttresses and heaven-pointing arches is an outward expression of man's soaring spirit and his longing for the eternal. In wood and stone, in girders and beams, man gives outward form and expression to the inner meanings of his life.

Eating is a sacrament, a sacrament of nature, and a sacrament of human life. It is a sacrament of nature because through it man incorporates in his body the life of nature, by which both soul and body are sustained on this earth. It is a sacrament of human life because eating a meal together is the commonest expression of our togetherness.

Man's whole life on earth is a sacrament. He lives by sacraments, by which we mean outward acts with inner meaning, material forms with spiritual significance. Man's whole personality is an image of him who made it: *the spirit of man is the candle of the Lord!* That is to say, through the nature of man we understand the nature of God. We, as children of God, are made in the likeness and image of the Father in heaven.

III

To the Church has been especially entrusted the sacramental principle for the nurture of the divine life in the soul of man. The sacraments are not of man's making but God's gift. The sacraments were instituted by Christ himself as "certain sure witnesses, and effectual signs of grace, and God's good will towards us, by the which he doth work invisibly in us, and doth not only quicken, but also strengthen and confirm our Faith in him."

Here again we see how God in the two principal sacraments uses the most common things of every day to impart himself to us: water, and bread and wine.

Through Holy Baptism we are incorporated into Christ, literally born again into the life which became manifest in Christ. Through faith we appropriate that life in the Church, that "as we grow in age, we may grow in grace, and in the knowledge of our Lord and Saviour, Jesus Christ."

Confirmation, the Laying on of Hands, is in a sense the fulfillment of Baptism, whereby, as we stand on the threshold of adulthood and renew our promises to Christ, we are assured of his help to keep our promises to him, assured of the strengthening of the "courage to be." And how could we be Christians without the promise of God's help?

In the Holy Communion, we are provided the means whereby our souls may be continually nourished by the Christ-life, whereby his presence is continually made real to us, whereby we receive the pledges and tokens of our eternal life.

The Church has always recognized certain lesser rites having the nature of sacraments, as for example, Holy

Matrimony. Herein, when we promise an immortal love to another human mortal, God promises that he will help us keep that promise. Again, how could we expect to keep such a promise without the help of God?

In Unction, the anointing of the sick with oil (or the laying on of hands), we are assured that *though the outward man decayeth the inner man is renewed day-by-day.*

In Penance, whereby we are encouraged to confess our sin, as well as our sins, we are made certain that nothing, especially no failure or defection on our part, can separate us from the love of God, which is in Christ Jesus our Lord.

Finally, in the Burial Office, the Church comes to us in the presence of death, and bids us to commit those we love but see no longer unto him, in whose hands they will be in safekeeping, and to sorrow not as those who have no hope, but to look with lively faith to that great day when we shall be reunited with them in the nearer presence of God.

And so from birth to death, God ministers to us through the sacramental life of the Church, and in all the crises of life, bids us to turn to him, who is the Lover of our souls, and in knowledge of whom we find our eternal life.

The Church comes to each of us with its offer of sacramental life, through which as *we draw nigh* unto God, *God draws nigh* unto us, and we come to know that his gracious hand is over all his works.

I.

The Preparation for Sacramental Living

SAMUEL J. WYLIE:

Holy Baptism ⮧   *1.*

All men dream of a better world than the one in which we live. We long for a life of personal freedom and happiness, for full stomachs and shared benefits, for dignity and creativity and spontaneity. We express it in political slogans: "one nation, indivisible, with liberty and justice for all." The idea captures the minds of artists and writers. Utopia, Erewhon, Shangri-la, stand alongside the vision of the City of God as evidence that Christians have no monopoly on the idea of human dignity and truly humane community.

Perhaps the most haunting artistic expression of that yearning in recent years is in one of the songs from the musical play *West Side Story*. Tony and Maria, young and in love, across the boundaries of New York's juvenile gang warfare, try to stop a fight by the intensity of their love for each other and their goodwill toward their neighbors. Not only does Tony fail in his mission, but he also is the means of murdering Maria's brother. In the resultant misery the two heartbroken lovers sing, "There's a place for us, some-

13

where; a time and place for us." While they sing, the ugly back-alley stage sets disappear, space and light spread over the scene, and the two rival gangs are amalgamated into a stately dance that catches up the members in its pattern of order and gracefulness. It cannot last, of course, and the actors and audience are soon pulled back to the brutal reality, not without tears and regrets for the lost vision of loveliness conjured up from the depths of the hearts of players and spectators alike.

What is the real world and the real humanity? Is it the humanity of our good dreams or of the sordid alleys, or of both? Are we fully human simply by the biological fact of our human ancestry? Can we be more human or less human according to the views we hold on the nature and destiny of man? Are slaves less human than free men? Is it possible that man may be depersonalized some day to the point where a being made in God's image ceases to exist and only a biochemical shell remains?

However we may answer these questions about man's essential nature, there can be no doubt that our present broken world makes it impossible simply to enter by birth into a common human brotherhood. We are black or white or Oriental. We are Eastern or Western in the global political struggle. Our close identification with some men precludes our close identification with all. No one is born into the Family of Man. That family is so torn and divided that each birth is a logistical statistic strengthening or weakening one group against another. No concept or practice defines mankind as a unity. There exists only the basic ability to distinguish man from the primates biologically, but with the rueful knowledge that in the twentieth century under fascism we have seen the last shreds of sanctity stripped from man as man and have watched one category of human hunted down and exterminated with the same moral detachment with which we eliminate undesirable rodents or insects.

The optimistic world of the liberal of the last century lies shattered around us. Of the common desire of practically all men for a good world there is no doubt. But there is no doubt either of the lengths to which men can and do go to bring destruction upon all in the effort to protect or augment the fortunes of a fraction of the whole.

One world organization alone maintains both the infinite worth of all men and the existence of a living community within time and space which embraces all men and all things. Christians are not alone in affirming the worth of man: they *are* alone in the audacious affirmation that God in Christ has reconciled not just some, but all mankind, to himself and unites them as they turn to him in a visible community which has order, structure, and continuity, being the agent of his unchanging purpose to restore all things to unity and purity of function in his service.

Christians do not come into the Church as a refuge from a humanity with which they are disillusioned, but in order to be fully human. This is a right which is denied them in the sectarianism of race, place, and class. The new life promised in Christ is not an alternative to normal human life; it *is* the normal life from which we have all fallen away. To become a Christian is not to join an aristocracy of the human race, the ultimate in spiritual excellence and exclusiveness. To become a Christian is to deny every kind of exclusiveness in a life commonly derived from God through Jesus Christ.

The thesis is well stated by F. D. Maurice:

The Universal Church, constituted in its Universal Head, exists to protest against a world which supposes itself to be a collection of incoherent fragments without a centre, which, where it reduces its practice to a maxim, treats every man as his own centre. The Church exists to tell the world of its true Centre, of the law of mutual sacrifice by which its parts are bound together. The Church exists to maintain the order of the nation and the order of the family, which this selfish practice and selfish maxim are continually threatening.[1]

Similarly, commenting on John 15:17-20, he said:

The one difference which we have already discovered between the world and those whom He chooses out of it, is that they confess a Centre, and that the world confesses none; that they desire to move, each in his own orbit, about this Centre, and that the world acknowledges only a revolution of each man about himself. The world, indeed, cannot realize its own principles. It must have companies, parties, sects—bodies acknowledging some principle of cohesion, aspiring after a kind of unity. Still, as a world, this is the description of it; and therefore, as a world, it must hate all who say, 'We are a society bound together, not by any law of our own, not by an election of our own, but by God's law and election.' [2]

"The World" in the biblical and negative sense, the same writer defines as

humanity trying to base itself on a falsehood, on a denial of its true constitution. It 'would have been torn in pieces by its individual factions,' did not this true constitution lie beneath it, this unconfessed bond of peace and fellowship. The world does not denote a society or an organization that is separate from the Church. It denotes a principle on which men are naturally in-

clined to organize their lives, a principle which is opposed to,
and a contradiction of, the order which has been prepared for
them by God. This false principle is at work everywhere and
always, in the Church itself as well as in the nation and the
family, but it is the special office of the Church to witness it by
witnessing to the truth.[3]

This is the world which St. Paul sharply condemns,
and about which our Lord says to his followers: "Ye shall
have tribulation: but be of good cheer; I have overcome
the world." (John 16:33) Out of *that* world, a world of
fragmentation and bondage, men and women redeemed
in Christ have been delivered. But, at the same time, they
have come out of it because "God so loved the world
[the creation] that he gave his only begotten Son" (John
3:16), and because "God was in Christ reconciling the world
unto himself" (II Cor. 5:19). We leave the broken *travesty*
of God's world (the rebellious world) in order to enter
the world of his redeeming, a world in the process of
restoration.

How God in Christ can do this is set forth tersely in
St. Paul's letter to the Colossian Church. He gives thanks
to the Father,

who has qualified us to share in the inheritance of the saints in
light. He has delivered us from the dominion of darkness and
transferred us to the kingdom of his beloved Son, in whom we
have redemption, the forgiveness of sins.

He is the image of the invisible God, the first-born of all
creation; for in him all things were created, in heaven and on
earth, visible and invisible, whether thrones or dominions or
principalities or authorities—all things were created through
him and for him. He is before all things, and in him all things
hold together. He is the head of the body, the church; he is the

beginning, the first-born from the dead, that in every thing he might be pre-eminent. For him all the fullness of God was pleased to dwell, and through him to reconcile to himself all things, whether on earth or in heaven, making peace by the blood of his cross.

And you, who once were estranged and hostile in mind, doing evil deeds, he has now reconciled in his body of flesh by his death, in order to present you holy and blameless and irreproach-able before him, provided that you continue in the faith . . . (Colossians 1:12-23 RSV)

This is the good news of redemption. The life-giving Word of the Father, by whose power the worlds were made, has lived among us, sharing our flesh and all the limitations of our humanity, and has by his human obedi-ence and humility even to the death set up a counter current against our disobedience and pride, restoring peace with God and hence within man and between men.

> O loving wisdom of our God!
> When all was sin and shame,
> A second Adam to the fight
> And to the rescue came.[4]

The New Testament sees the work of redemption as accomplished. It is attested by the resurrection of Christ from the dead. The solidarity of mankind in rebellion is matched by the solidarity of mankind brought into the life in Christ. Those who acknowledge his lordship and who share his life do not, therefore, leave the fallen human race. They are welded together by a common life to become intercessors for their brothers, agents of reconciliation, the continuation in time and space of our Lord's own human obedience and love.

Individuals converted to God, as they have come to trust him in Jesus Christ, come into this common life through Baptism. Conversion is a personal and human experience. It may be gradual or it may be dramatic. Baptism is God's action, through the Church, in which the converted individual is caught up or grafted into the Body of Christ and made a participant in the Life of the Body. That Life is Christ's own, shared through the fellowship. The New Testament is full of this imagery. Our Lord is quoted as saying: "I am the vine, and ye are the branches." (St. John 15:5) St. Paul uses the figure of the Body possessed of many organs all deriving life from the Head, who is Christ. St. Paul and the First Epistle of Peter use the metaphor of a living temple in which Christians are fitted as stones in relation to a chief cornerstone which is Christ. In all New Testament imagery, as in the Old Testament from which it derives, to be a child of God is to be a member of the people of God. Individuals who by God's gift of faith have turned from disobedience, accepted God's forgiveness in Jesus Christ, and acknowledged him as Lord are grafted, adopted, incorporated into the community of the Holy Spirit, the Church, by Baptism. In an apt vulgarism a contemporary theologian has said that in Baptism we are "plugged into the circuit" of God's power in the Church.

We cannot come into the fullness of the fully human life in Christ without repudiating our idolatrous loyalty to the fragmented and self-centered life we have been leading. We must die to the old life to be reborn into the new. "Marvel not," our Lord reminds us, "that I say unto thee, Ye must be born again." "Except a man be born of water

and of the Spirit, he cannot enter into the kingdom of God."
(John 3:5, 7) St. Paul develops the figure as a death and
resurrection. "Do you now know that all of us who have
been baptized into Christ Jesus were baptized into his
death? We were buried therefore with him by baptism
into death, so that as Christ was raised from the dead by
the glory of the Father, we too might walk in newness of
life." (Romans 6:3, 4)

The theology of the New Testament, and some of its
language, is reflected in the office of Holy Baptism in the
Book of Common Prayer. The candidate for baptism is
asked: "Dost thou renounce the devil and all his works,
the vain pomp and glory of the world, with all covetous
desires of the same, and the sinful desires of the flesh, so
that thou wilt not follow, nor be led by them?" He is then
led to confess his faith in Christ as Saviour and Lord, and
in the Christian Faith as contained in the Apostles' Creed.
He promises to keep God's commandments by God's help.
The officiant prays and the congregation assents by its
Amen to the following petitions:

> O merciful God, grant that like as Christ died and rose again
> so this thy Servant may die to sin and rise to newness of life.
> Grant that all sinful affections may die in him, and that all
> things belonging to the Spirit may live and grow in him.
> Grant that he may have power and strength to have victory,
> and to triumph, against the devil, the world, and the flesh.

After these solemn and lonely actions (solitary as death
must always be), and after the blessing of the water to its
holy purpose, the candidate is named. He will be anonymous and alone no longer. He is baptized by that name
in God's own Name and emerges from the water to be

received into the congregation of Christ's flock, signed with his Cross, challenged to endure his discipline. A prayer of thanksgiving that the newly baptized person is regenerate and grafted into the body of Christ's Church follows, and the service ends on a note of universality. The officiating minister quotes St. Paul:

The Almighty God, the Father of our Lord Jesus Christ, of whom the whole family in heaven and earth is named; Grant you to be strengthened with might by his Spirit in the inner man; that Christ dwelling in your hearts by faith, ye may be filled with all the fulness of God.

If we turn from language to the rite of Baptism itself, we will see that all of the elements discussed above are included in the symbolism of the ritual action, and appeal beyond reason to far more fundamental levels of being.

Water as a symbol speaks to the depths of primitive and sophisticated folk alike. We are accustomed to thinking of life as having originated in the seas. We are aware that each new human life is cradled and nurtured in the waters of the womb, and that we carry in our bodies the saltiness of the seas themselves. The Jungian psychologists tell us that water is the most common archetypal image of the unconscious

and that a descent into the water is normally a symbolic description of a new penetration into those deeper and more mysterious fecundities from which a true creativity can be derived. Other elements are associated with water in this dim realm of the unconscious—the void, darkness, death, silence, loneliness—but water is the symbol which gathers all these associations together in a comprehensive way.

F. W. Dillistone summarizes the primitive and psycho-analytic significance of water under three headings:

(1) Water from the heavens has been regarded as possessing life-giving properties and therefore to be sprinkled with water means to receive renewal of life.

(2) Water gushing from the earth has been regarded as issuing from the womb of the Earth-Mother and to be plunged in this water has been regarded as a means of gaining the gift of immortality.

(3) Still water, the water of darkness, has also in some way been associated with the womb: to descend into this water is to return to the source of creativity for renewal of life.

Thus in and through the rite of Christian initiation there is the possibility of touching the deepest level of the 'general memory' or the 'collective unconscious.' As Louis Beirnaert has convincingly shown, early Christian theologians delighted to speak of baptism in terms of maternal images. 'You have plunged thrice in the water,' writes Cyril of Jerusalem, 'and have come forth again. In the water, as during the night, you have seen nothing. In coming forth you have found yourself in the brightness of day. At the same time you died and were born, and this wholesome water has become for you both a tomb and a mother.' [5]

Here is poetic evidence of the Christian affirmation that in Baptism we turn back, far back, along the path of human social experience to a restoration of the unity we dimly remember before the fall.

Another bit of water imagery captured the imagination of the ancients. The Jews, certainly, were no sailors and hated the sea. They saw it as a symbol of chaos. With their neighbors they thought of monsters or dragons inhabiting the depths. To cross the seas or to enter and defeat the monster was a symbol of ultimate victory or deliverance.

Bestir thyself, O arm of the Eternal,
bestir thyself and don thy might!
Bestir thyself as in the days of old,
   in ages of the past!
    Didst thou not shatter the Rahab
    and pierce the Dragon through?
Didst thou not once dry up the sea,
   and waters of the mighty deep,
and make the ocean-depths a path
    for ransomed men to pass across? [6]

Dillistone goes on to comment:

As Mr. W. H. Auden has pointed out in the deeply interesting study of water symbolism, the general view of the sea and of man's journeyings on it has tended to vary from age to age. Man may face the waters in a spirit of adventure, in a spirit of compulsion, in a spirit of *hubris* (pride) or in a spirit of sober determination. Always, however, the voyage separates him from his former existence; he will emerge from it either hardened and toughened or purified and enlightened. [7]

Cyril of Jerusalem, referring to the deliverance of the Jews at the Red Sea, says to his catechumens: "The tyrant has pursued the ancient people even to the sea; you too, this impudent demon and prince of evil has pursued even to the waters of salvation. The one was drowned in the sea, the other vanishes in the water of salvation." [8]

Myth and poetry here come to St. Paul's side to express the reality that in conversion and Baptism men pass from darkness into light, from sickness to health, and from the kingdom of Satan to the kingdom of Christ.

One further and obvious bit of symbolism remains to be observed. Baptism is cleansing, washing, a purification. Perhaps because the figure is so obvious, perhaps because such is the moralistic temper of much of Christendom, moral reform has overmuch dominated our teaching and thinking on baptism. To be sure, moral reform is a part of the Gospel, but it is a pale substitute for the defeat of hell's dominion and the restoration of unity to which both the New Testament and the ancient symbolism bear witness.

To be baptized, then, is to enter into an intensely personal experience of self-renunciation, to "pass through the waters," to die with Christ, and to emerge a member of a community, a stone in a living temple, an organ within a body, a branch on a vine. To present oneself for baptism is to stand naked and alone and, in a sense, anonymous before the community of redeemed Man; and to be clothed, adopted, and given a name.

It is in this experience that we come to understand why the children of believers must also be baptized. In a pagan pre-Christian society such as that of the first century, one was counted as belonging either to the kingdom of this world or to the kingdom of Christ. There was no comfortable middle ground of conventional Christendom. To be Christ's was to be a candidate for martyrdom. To be Caesar's was to be an enemy of Christ. In such a society Christians had an option either to raise their children *within* the community of Christ, wrapping them in its concern and exposing them to its power before the child was old enough to define his own experience and make his own confession of faith, or to raise him as a pagan and an enemy of the Lord. There could be only one choice.

The situation is less dramatic today, but in essence it remains unchanged. Little children in Baptist homes (and

in other Christian bodies that restrict Baptism to adults)
pray to Christ, love Christ, serve Christ according to their
childish ability from their earliest days. They thus live
the life of the community and are in an unofficial way part
of it for years before the actual incorporation takes place.
If Christians were suddenly to be persecuted in our land,
parents would certainly not count their unbaptized children
as pagans, even though they were in danger of suffering
because of the Christian tag placed upon them. By far the
majority of Christians bring their children to baptism at
the first opportunity that they may share in the life of the
Spirit mediated through the Christian community. On the
strength of the sponsors' faith the Church receives them
in trust that the individual commitment will follow. We
cannot ourselves share in eternal life and postpone to the
age of twelve our children's part in it. We cannot count
ourselves as Christians and our children as pagans or neu-
trals. Like the Jews before us, we bring our children into
the life of the redeemed community of which we are a
part and make our spiritual inheritance theirs as well. Because Baptism truly admits them into the community of
the Holy Spirit, the Body whose life is Christ, it is not
only the exhibition but the conferral of grace. That is to
say, God's good will is not only promised and declared, but
his love expressed in and through the Church surrounds
and possesses the child at the moment of his reception
into the Church through Baptism.

The strength of the child's Christian experience and
the depth of his spiritual life becomes directly dependent
on the vitality of the life of the Church in his parish and
in his home. The rite of Baptism abstracted from the life

in the community can be near-magic. But Baptism as the reaching out of the people of God and of Christ himself to enfold in love and prayer a new soul is the outward and visible sign of inner participation in a new life. Baptism, like all the sacraments of God's love, is an assurance that when we turn to God in repentance and faith he acts decisively in us and through us, and the validity of the work of redemption rests not on our worthiness, nor on the strength of our faith, but on his power and his love. He does not fail his people.

Luther, when plagued with doubts and despair about his own spiritual life, would write and hold before him the words, "I have been baptized." It was an assurance that the life in Christ depends on Christ; that the work God has begun, God will continue. Here is encouragement for all of us. For us men and for our salvation Christ came down. He has reconciled us to the Father by the offering of himself on the Cross. He has destroyed the power of death by his rising from the dead. In our baptism he has led us back through the waters to the restoration of our true humanity. He has ransomed us from the kingdom of darkness and established us in the kingdom of light. He has washed us and made us clean. He intends that we shall be like himself. Nothing can prevent this process from taking place in us except pride or despair. No amount of failure, no amount of doubt, no low estimate of our own worth can deny the fact that we are baptized—we are the Lord's. We are holy by our association with the Holy One. "By grace are ye saved through faith; and that not of yourselves: It is the gift of God: Not of works, lest any man should boast." (Ephesians 2:8, 9)

Herein also is the democracy of the people of God. There are diversities of gifts within the Body. There are specialized functions also. There are national characteristics that adorn and enrich its life, and will continue to do so through all eternity. The book of Revelation describes the city of God in heaven as a place where "the nations of them which are saved shall walk in the light of it; and the kings of the earth do bring their glory and honour into it." (Revelation 21:24) But the loftiest of the kings and the humblest of citizens, the noblest of the saints and the most wretched sinners have only one claim to membership in the Church: they have confessed their faith in Jesus Christ the Lord, have been baptized into him, and live by his life.

Preparing for the Sacramental Life ৯ 2.

Almost everyone, I suppose, who has read Brother Lawrence's conversations and letters, called *The Practice of
the Presence of God,* has deeply admired this good brother,
who, working amid the pots and pans of a busy monastery
kitchen, made those hours of toil hours of profound spiritual
experience. We remember the account he gives of the few
minutes which changed his life. It seems that one winter
day, when he was eighteen years old, Brother Lawrence
stood looking at a bare tree. He realized that before long
it would be covered with leaves; then the flowers and
fruit would appear. This is the kind of miracle we see a
thousand times and take for granted. Brother Lawrence
did not. He told a friend about it long afterwards. He said
that as he looked, he "received a high view of the providence and power of God which has never since been
effaced from his soul. That this view had . . . kindled in

him such a love for God that he could not tell whether it had increased in above forty years he had lived since."

To this man, more than sixty years old when he recounted the experience, the event was as vivid as on the day it occurred, because he had seen it with his inner eyes and it had become a part of his whole being.

Although we know of such happenings in the lives of giant souls in the Church, we must remember that they are not withheld from ordinary men and women. To each one of us there come moments in life when we see with a startling clarity; we find our horizons widened, we see a glimpse of truth we have not understood before. Sometimes we let these times drift by, and they are forgotten. At others, when the world is momentarily transfigured, we live so intensely and are granted such a clear flash of vision that, like Brother Lawrence, we are never the same again.   We have attained to a higher level of reality, or, to put it another way, we are more fully alive.

These moments of clearer vision and deeper understanding may come at times of deep sorrow or great joy: when we love or when we worship; when we see or hear great beauty; when we are thankful or when we forgive and are forgiven; when we are creating with mind or hand; or when we are working at what we believe to be the most commonplace task. The moment will come unexpectedly. The important thing is that it shall be recognized, cherished, and acted upon.

One thing seems certain, and that is, although we cannot predict when these experiences of fuller life will come, we can be sure there is one time when they will not come— that is, when we are worrying about ourselves, our little wants and hurts and frustrations. We need to go right out of ourselves to enter into another life, to look with awe and reverence at something or someone, or to do some simple thing for love.

On the night of our Lord's birth, the innkeeper's wife in Stephen Vincent Benet's play, *A Child Is Born*, tells of her life up to that moment.[1] She says she has been afraid to follow the moments of vision, and she suddenly realizes that she had been only half alive. She tells them,

> Life can be
> Lost without vision, but not lost by death,
> Lost by not caring, willing, going on
> Beyond the ragged edge of fortitude
> To something more—something no man has seen . . .
> Rise up! The loves we had were not enough.
> Something is loosed to change the shaken world
> And with it we must change!

This woman understood that until then she had been only half-alive. If we are only half-alive, we are half-dead. Can it be true that if we do not follow the vision of which she speaks, do not enter into the fullness of life God intends for us, we do not know what it means to live? To most thoughtful people there comes a moment in life when we become conscious of the fact that *we are*. We are suddenly aware of our existence and the stupendous thought comes to us: "I *am*—I am a person—and I am really here." To some that knowledge comes very early. Later—often much too late—another reality dawns: our time is not our own to use as we please, and the part of our existence which we call our earthly life is shortened every day by twenty-four hours. The very fact that we exist means that we possess the shining gift of life, given to us by God. When this truth comes to us, we are even more alive than before. We begin to ask great questions, and we say, "I am. I shall continue to be. I am one of God's creatures and he cares about his creation."

Not every one learns this fact in a crisis, but some do. I know of a man who was felling a tree. Something went wrong and he found himself under the bulldozer, partly crushed. He lay very still while his companion ran for help. His life was spared, and when he had recovered from his injuries, he was a changed person. He continues to say to his friends, "I don't know exactly what has happened to me, but I can't get rid of one thought: *I am alive!* Every day I am happy and grateful for my existence. I never thought about it before." This man is never guilty of looking for something "to pass away the time," or even more tragically "to kill time."

Our theme is "Preparing for the Sacramental Life," and part of that preparation is a thankfulness for life itself. The solemn miracle and joyful fact is that we are here and alive, able to worship God, to love and enjoy him and each other. We can rejoice in the words of the third morning prayer in Family Prayer: "And since it is of thy mercy, O gracious Father, that *another day* is added to our lives . . ." (BCP, p. 588)

The innkeeper's wife realized one other thing on the night the angels sang, "Glory to God in the highest." She knew that until then she had been missing the *glory*—what she called the "shining change"—which is there all the time behind the visible world. She was coming very close to one of the definitions of worship given by Evelyn Underhill: "Worship is the adoring acknowledgement of all that lies beyond us—the glory that fills heaven and earth." It is God himself who leads us across the frontier which lies between us and this larger universe. It is through the new eyes of worship that we come to see that all of life is penetrated by God, and the glory which was always present at last becomes apparent. Sacramental life is life opened up to God so that his glory may come in.

Now there are some who, when they hear the words "sacramental life" may say, "I am sure it is a beautiful and poetic idea, but it is not for us who have to bear the brunt of the wear and tear of ordinary life. It is a fine thing for those who have time and opportunity to think about it— the clergy, for instance, and professional religious, the very good people, the spiritual élite. It is an excellent thing for the special group that attends the 8 o'clock service on Saints' days—for older people, too, and invalids—but not for the practical, down-to-earth men and women who have to get the world's work done."

There are others who will also agree that they will begin to live more fully, and give more time to their devotional life when their children have grown, or when they move to another neighborhood or change their work or retire—but not *now*. These people are making a tragic mistake. The sacramental life is for sinners, which means every one of us. And while the lives we are living have meaning in eternity, they are lived *now*, in the present moment. We must live in the acceptance of our present circumstances, which does not mean they will never change, but that we are called to live fully in the minute-to-minute events and relationships of our everyday existence. We cannot put off the fact of the present. "The soul cannot be united to God," says De Caussade in his wonderful book *Abandonment to the Divine Providence,* "except in the fulfillment of the present moment"; and again, "The present moment is always filled with infinite treasures; it contains more than you are capable of receiving . . . O Love, will men never see that thou meetest them at every step, while they seek thee hither and thither where thou art not?"

If we are to come into our inheritance as members of the Body of Christ, we must participate, as fully as we are able, in the eucharistic worship of the Church. To do this we cannot be spectators who stand afar off. Outward conformity in worship, regular churchgoing, and much giving of time and substance to "church work" are not necessarily an indication that we have entered as fully as we are able into the sacramental life.

Through Holy Baptism we die with Christ and rise into the new life; through the Holy Communion we receive the gift of God's own self, by which he enables us to live in sustained contact with him. He supports and fulfills us and gives us the fullness of life for which we seek. But we must be prepared to *respond* to his action, the offering of his Love, his very self, which we call *grace.*

We may now describe this life in Christ, as we have considered it, thus:

The sacramental life is the life in which the individual *accepts* the offering of God's own self through God-chosen means. Through the simple acts of washing and feeding, made holy in Baptism and in the Eucharist, a Christian discovers his unique relationship with God as a member of the Body of Christ. A life opened up to God and transformed by him is called the sacramental life.

How, then, may we best prepare for it? And because all Christians are teachers—whether they are aware of it or not—we must also ask what is the most helpful way to answer the questions of newcomers, both young and old, as they prepare to take their place in the full sacramental life of the Church.

Although many people are not aware of it, we all are sacramentalists. The sacramental principle is like a thread running through the entire pattern of our existence. In our everyday lives, outward and visible things express what is inward and spiritual. This may be seen in a simple gesture of greeting and the imposing celebration of a national festival; in a postage stamp or a World Fair. It may be seen in a thousand humble customs in our homes.

The word "sacrament" has a very long history. It is worth tracing right back through the centuries when, in classical Latin, *sacramentum* meant "a sacred pledge between man and man." The sacraments of the Church are still a sacred pledge: God fulfilling his promises to man. Spiritual reality is brought to us through material means because that is the way we are created to receive it. Those who think of the whole physical world as evil speak of Christianity as a "spiritual religion." This is a heresy which has terrible effects, not only on the way we think of ourselves and our fellow men, but also on our attitude to eucharistic worship. Instead of understanding the Real Presence of Christ in the Holy Communion, he is thought of as a misty figure, hovering over the altar. Here is an example of the necessity for *right belief* in our preparation for the sacramental life. Faith and knowledge go hand in hand in helping us to *respond* to the love of God.

When we come to understand the sacramental principle more clearly, it is easier to see—and to help others to see—why God chose two humble, universal necessities, our need to be washed and to be fed, as the basis for his two great sacraments, Holy Baptism and Holy Communion. Von Hügel reminds us that the saints have found in the Holy Communion, "The Infinite first condescending to the finite, so that the finite may rise towards the Infinite." [2] Jesus Christ himself has been called "The Greatest Sacrament," for he is the supreme creation, the perfect union of creature and Creator. And the wonder of all wonders is that God not only dwelt among us sacramentally in the days of his flesh, but that he continues to be with us, making himself known in the Breaking of the Bread. He remakes us, and we become what we are, members of his Body, his new creation. Some day we may learn to see that all the world is being created anew, that every living reality has a meaning which transcends this earth. We shall gradually see more of the "shining change," the glory. We shall see the whole cosmos as a revelation of divine love.

Truth so astonishing is sometimes hard to accept, especially when we become tired and bitter and earth-bound. We say, "Wouldn't it be wonderful if it were so!" We cannot bring ourselves to accept the unbelievable generosity of God. We have not the trust that two missionaries in different parts of the world describe in their converts: that of the African woman who, on hearing the Gospel, said, "I always knew there must be a God like that!" or that of the Chinese convert who declared, "I have always known him, but I did not know his name." We say enviously, "I wish I had her faith," forgetting that not only is faith (or trust) a gift which grows as we move into the unknown, treading the paths worn by those who have gone ahead of us, but that it is strengthened through knowledge of God. That knowledge comes through our participation in the worship and work of the Church, and part of our Christian work is reading. Preparing for the sacramental life—and when we come to think of it, does not this preparation go on for the whole of our lives?—includes a growing knowledge of the Bible and of Christian faith and practice. This does not mean scanning a few Bible verses before we fall off to sleep at night and feeling that we have done something noble for God by giving him our last weary minutes; it means a little discipline which we might include, in a moment, when we think about our rule of life.

We are looking for ways of opening the door so that the King of Glory may come into our lives. We have considered the seriousness of wrong attitudes and beliefs. What other barriers stand in the way?

We shall be moving away from our central purpose if we try to find answers to the battery of excuses offered by those who deliberately choose to stay outside the Church. Some of these are an expression of honest doubt; some not. Instead, let us look at a few of the *hidden* stumbling blocks which lie in the way of many regular churchgoers. For it is possible for us as churchgoers to cherish disbelief because we are afraid to admit that we have doubts. In order to live more fully "in Christ," however, we need to bring our hidden doubts into the daylight and face them bravely.

They can end by being a way into the sacramental life. God knows about them, even if we do not. We can pray, "Help thou my unbelief."

We all bring into adult life some of the childish notions about God which may have come to us through poor teaching, unhappy experiences, bad art, or through those who have given us the impression that religion is dull, that it consists in keeping rules which are always too difficult. Some have never learned to *enjoy* God. This first observation is tied to what we have said previously. We need to grow in our knowledge of the faith; and if necessary, we can turn to a priest who will direct us. Worship is a relationship of love and trust; and we can, through the grace of God, overcome the doubts and fears that beset us. An adult man or woman meets sorrow as well as joy. The Christian has never been promised a smooth and comfortable life; we all meet pain and rejection as well as fulfillment and gladness. In the sacramental life we receive the power to face doubt and indifference. These stumbling blocks may be transformed into steppingstones.

As our life of worship and prayer develops, the less likely are we to be overthrown by another obstacle, that is, the tendency we have to put the stress of our thought on ourselves, on what we want and feel and are doing. We do this in such a way that in our ridiculous self-centeredness we put ourselves in the spotlight and to the front of the stage; and God, hidden somewhere behind the scenes, is called in to attend to our needs, particularly in emergencies, after which we are likely to dismiss him. George Herbert wrote a poem about this. He described his own behavior and said, "I would not use a friend as I use thee."

It is the same self-regarding tendency which makes us try to bend God's will to our own, and to be disappointed in him if he does not comply with our wishes. An Eastern prayer gives us perspective here:

> My desires are many and my cry is pitiful;
> But ever thou hast upheld me with wise refusals.

When we thank God for his "wise refusals" we are beginning to grow up.

We are the victims of modern teaching which so often puts man and his little adventures in the foreground. And I believe it is true that the Western Church has tended to be more man-centered than God-centered for three or four centuries. The emphasis has been on man progressing towards perfection rather than on God raising him to perfection. Individual growth has been stressed rather than worship. We are sinful, but our preoccupation with sin and separation can be a disguised form of selfishness. When we come into the presence of God at the altar and remember that we are made in his image, we can fill our hearts with thankfulness, instead of indulging in what has been called "the cheap luxury of melancholy." When we come in penitence and faith, we can respond to the love of God, but there will not be room for him to stay in our lives if we return to meditate *chiefly* on our sin instead of his righteousness. I have always rejoiced in the advice given by a spiritual director to a lady overzealous in self-accusation and, therefore, spending too little time in discovering the glory of God: "There is nothing very interesting or unusual about sin. In spite of it all, God loves us and holds on to us." Just think of that! The Creator cares about his creatures and sustains them, and at the heart of the universe, in spite of all the misery, is the conquering power and tenderness and righteousness of God in Christ. We remember the Collect for Easter Day: "He has delivered us from the power of the enemy . . . that we may evermore live with him in the joy of his resurrection."

There is no one who has not had to meet another obstacle—the problem of evil. It is an old, stubborn question which rears its head before us all. We have dark times when we fear that evil is stronger than good. Our faith wavers and there is a period of unreality in our worship. We are angry with God. Christianity does not pretend to have an explanation to the problem of evil, but there is an answer. We can have faith in the love of God because he became man. He took our evil upon himself and suffered death. He triumphed over death and changed our relationship with God forever, sharing with us the gift of eternal life. As we surrender our self-sufficiency, he continues to give himself in the sacramental life.

The contemporary poet Alan Paton describes the longing for God which we bring to the altar thus:

Such was the bondage of the earth, such was the misery,
Such was the reaching out, such was the separation,
That my Lord tore the curtain from the skies, and in compassion
He took upon himself all angry things, the thorn, the nail, the
    utter separation
And spake such words as made me tremble, and laid his yoke
    upon me . . .
I said in my heart to him, I who in sins and doubts and in my
    grievous separation reach out my hands,
Reach out thy hands and touch me, O most Holy One.[3]

Another barrier we need to break down is our delight in doing good works, and praying for our neighbors afar off to the exclusion of those with whom we live and work. We must come to the altar not as individuals making a private communion, but as people sharing a common corporate life. When we worship God, our brothers and sisters are beside us. We cannot learn to love God unless we learn to love our fellow men. Saint Augustine gives us very clear teaching here: "The love of God comes first in order of command, but the love of our neighbor first in order of practice. Love, therefore, your neighbor; and behold in yourself that by which you love your neighbor; and looking at that you will see, as best you may, God."

We often find it hard to remember that our neighbors are, among others, those who sit across from us at meal time in our home, and those irritating people we meet in our daily work. It is much easier to love our distant brethren, or the more dramatically interesting "problem people" we serve through committees than our close friends and relations. Mrs. Jellaby in Dickens' *Bleak House* is an outstanding example of this. You will remember her zeal in serving good causes, while her children had little of her time, and her husband "was often seen to open his mouth but seldom heard to speak."

The mystery is that as we learn to love those around us, our love for God grows too. One priest I know, when he teaches about the Holy Communion, says, "Come and receive God's offering of himself. We are all slow to learn; but one day when you leave the altar, you will be able to get as far as the first pew without thinking ill of your neighbors; and then it will be the third pew and so on,

until at long last you may be able to carry the love of God
right out into the world."

One last factor in our preparation for the sacramental
life; this is the offering of ourselves. When we come to
the altar we say, "Here we offer and present unto thee, O
Lord, our selves . . ." It seems to me that while we cannot
become what we are without God's grace, we stand in the
way of his entry if we *refuse to be what we are*. A man
offers his manhood to God. A woman offers her womanhood. For a moment I would like to speak of the role of
women.

At a time when civilization desperately needs what
women have to contribute to it, we find instead much imi-
tation of men, much unnecessary competition with them
(for women have their own particular gifts) and a rejection
of the very differences which constitute their strength. In
fact, many women rebel against having been created
women.

Of course, women have no desire to return to the days
before their emancipation—too many wrongs were righted.
I simply want to state that as a sex, women frequently
forget their vocation, which is the creation, preservation,
and protection of life and the relationships between lives.
A worldly career which gives no opportunity to use these
gifts may harden and embitter. Women have also lost sight
of the three relative superiorities attributed to them: their
ability to be "guardians of mercy, defenders of life, inspiration for sacrifice." Many women dislike being women;
homemaking and bringing up a family is seen as something
to be endured.

Men and women were created to complement, not

compete with, each other. Indeed, sometimes women lose sight of the very gifts which should enable them to enjoy womanhood, simply because they forget that they possess them. Even those called to a career in the outside world need not discard their peculiar talents and imitate men.

Farseeing people are now reminding us that the moral tone of a whole civilization depends upon its women, because women choose the terms on which they shall be loved. Moreover, while they hate to be called irrational, we cannot deny that the majority of women have minds that function with an emphasis on the intuitive, symbolic side of life. The contemporary writer Gerald Vann is one of those who are trying to awaken us. In his book *The Water and the Fire,* he says: "If a woman neglects her own particular birthright, both man and woman suffer, the whole human race suffers." [4] He begs women, because they are closer to nature and the material world than men, to bring back the reverence for all created things which our world is losing, because of its preoccupation with technology. Surely, as they enter the sacramental life, where the natural and the supernatural meet, where the seen and the unseen are so wonderfully mingled, they can find a reason for being what they are and rejoice in it. In the Liturgy creation is once more lifted up to the Creator. There we discover who we are, what God intends us to be; and through his grace we go back into the world to *become* what he intends us to be.

There has been much of the "how" as well as the "why" in our thinking. We can sum it up in a simple rule of life. The pattern for our entrance into the sacramental life is found within the Liturgy itself. The central meeting place is in the Holy Communion. God the Holy Spirit teaches through his Church: priest and people, the whole Family of God worshipping together. We hear the proclamation of the Atoning Life in epistle, gospel, creed, and sermon; then we enter into the New Life, when Christ repeats the ascension in us and we have a foretaste of existence in the Kingdom. Through his grace we receive reality.

Here is our first rule: regular participation in the eucharistic worship of the Church. Then, through prayer and study we can learn to respond more fully to what God offers. We can make a place somewhere in our busy day— and most of us lead busy, even driven, lives—for prayer and study. If we say this is impossible, we can discover how much time we find for lesser things. Good books are recommended to us. We can begin with them—in the present moment!

We can cultivate the habit of thankfulness for God and for each other. We can look daily at our lives and see how many gifts we have which were given by God. We can look for God everywhere, and we may come to say of what we thought were commonplace days:

"Thou dost beset me behind and before, and layest thy hand upon me.
Such knowledge is too wonderful for me. . . .
Whither shall I go from thy Spirit? Or whither shall I flee from thy presence? . . .
If I take the wings of the morning and dwell in the uttermost parts of the sea,
Even there thy hand shall lead me, and thy right hand shall hold me." (Psalm 139 RSV)

When we remember this, we shall bring real thanksgiving to the altar.

If we have felt no thankfulness before, how can we suddenly offer it to God on Sundays and Saints' days? We can train ourselves to see the little sacramentals of life as a preparation for The Sacrament. One woman who understood this wrote:

> I am aware
> As I go commonly sweeping the stair . . .
> I am aware of the splendour that ties
> All the things of the earth with the things of the skies.[5]

This is the glory that lies behind the world we see, the glory that fills heaven and earth. We can train ourselves to ask, "Have I allowed fatigue, illness, or some emotion to blot out the glory of God?" Every time we see "the shining change" and are thankful, our preparation for the sacramental life continues. We learn to say with the psalmist: "Thou dost guide me with thy counsel and afterward thou wilt receive me to glory. . . . it is good to be near God." (Psalm 73 RSV)

EDWARD N. WEST:

Confirmation ❧ 3.

The Western mind has a basic taste for precise definition and the separation of ideas. We are, nowadays, forced to treat as separate, things which in the early Church were part of a continuous process. You will realize that our Lenten Season comes from the preparation of catechumens for Baptism. These people brought up in a pagan world had to learn Christian ethics. They had first to learn the Law of the Old Testament, the simple rights and wrongs for decent people, before they could go on to the finer points of the Spirit. The Spirit was overlaid on the Law; and the Spirit, while it does away with the Law, does away with it only after one has learned to do the Law. These pagans, in the company of their sponsors, were trained by fasting and prayer and lections, so that by the end of Lent they could receive Baptism, Confirmation, and First Communion—in one continuous service. This was done on Easter Even, late at night, so that when the Holy Communion itself took place, it would be in the early hours of the first day of the week—the time the Gospel assigns to the Resurrection.

In the course of time, the Western Church found itself in a strange position. It was anxious to continue this uniform service of Baptism, Confirmation, and Holy Communion, but actually was unable to do so. In the Eastern world the dioceses were very small. The Eastern world was an urban world. Therefore, any sizable town, any sizable city, had its own bishop. It was no problem at all for the bishop to be at hand, for the bishop to confirm, and for everything to continue in the ancient pattern. In the West, however, particularly in the barbarian areas, the dioceses were tremendous in size. It was impossible for a bishop to be in his cathedral and have all his new people with him at the appropriate period—it was physically impossible. Thus gradually the Western Church, for practical reasons, ended up by separating services which had once been continuous.

Baptism, first in barbarian areas and then only eventually in the East, came to be administered generally to children. This had not been true in the early Church. Baptism, after all, was costly business. It meant that a man could be called upon to lay down his life for Christ. If today you see the tombs of the Martyrs, you must remember that these are the monuments of people who paid the entire cost of loving their Lord. The extent of infant baptism in the early Church is unknown. Some years ago (on one side of this particular argument) men used to insist that one could find on the tombs accounts of little children aged one, two, three, ten, or eleven; this was a quite convincing argument, except for the somewhat unfortunate fact that the years recorded only dated from the date of baptism. Thus a man baptized at the age of forty and dying at the age of forty-one would be counted as one-year-old. This argument did not provide the support hoped for. It found its support rather in the great age recorded for some Christians. If a man had "served Christ for eighty years," one could readily believe that he had been baptized as a child!

In the West, however, there is no doubt that baptism of infants came to be the universal custom. Confirmation, hopefully, would then be done at some period when the child could be brought to the bishop and some responsibility might be assumed.

It is characteristic of the Western world that confirmation is associated with responsibility. This is not true of the Eastern Church. In the Eastern Church still, a tiny baby is brought in, is baptized, and confirmed. Their service of confirmation is called *Chrismation*, which means anointing with oil which has been blessed by the bishop. The result is that the child is immediately attached to the larger Church and, as a "complete" Christian, enters into its full life by being administered Holy Communion then and there. An Orthodox child is brought up with (and on) Holy Communion; for Orthodoxy this is the normal way. On one Sunday in the year, generally in September (near the Feast of the Elevation of the Holy Cross), the children are brought to make their communions. Frankly, though this is so alien to us, it is nevertheless one of the most tender sights in the world to see—mothers carrying up their children, the godparents standing close by, and the bishop or the priest solemnly giving the Holy Mysteries to Christ's little child, a child growing up in Christ's family.

That is not our pattern. Our pattern is to require the bishop personally to administer the Laying on of Hands. In medieval times, due to distance and misunderstanding, Confirmation almost completely disappeared. One of the scandals of the Middle Ages was the neglect of Confirmation. St. Hugh of Lincoln was regarded as a very great and particularly holy bishop, due to the fact that he bothered to get off horseback when he confirmed. The more remarkable thing is that he got there at all, because the whole pattern of the Middle Ages was against bothering with Confirmation. It always comes as a tremendous shock to us that the final rubric in our Confirmation office—the one which is often used without too much charity, the one which reads, "There shall be none admitted to the Holy Communion until such time as he be confirmed . . ."—was not the result of rows with Presbyterians in the Puritan Commonwealth, but rather the result of the medieval neglect of Confirmation. That rubric was from the Sarum manual. It is the work of Archbishop Peckham, who died in the year 1292! In 1280 the Archbishop had complained of the numberless people, grown old in evil days, who had not yet received the grace of Confirmation.

Sacchetti, an Italian contemporary of Chaucer, speaks of a good many who did not even feel certain of having been baptized. In the thirteenth century, in the Diocese of Noyon, out of a population of 900,000, more than 100,000 had died unconfirmed in one ten-year period. The figures in all medieval accounts are exaggerated—but the *propor-*

tion is not. The proportion is accurate, and it is a shocking account. Because of this separation of Baptism, Confirmation, and Holy Communion in the Western Church, one finds on the continent of Europe the practice of having First Communion prior to Confirmation. This has not proved an unmixed blessing to the Roman Church. One of the distinguished Roman liturgiologists complains that First Communion has become "the sacrament of the great apostasy." What he means is that grown children make their communion, and never again show up, even to be confirmed. I am informed by my Roman colleagues that this is still true, and true even in this country. The result for them is that the all-important thing is First Communion, and Confirmation is at best an optional service.

For the Anglican, Confirmation matters most terribly. This is partly because as a Church we suffered so dreadfully at the time of the Puritan Commonwealth. The Archbishop of Canterbury, William Laud, was beheaded; some of the bishops went to the Tower of London; some were imprisoned during the entire period; and some of our clergy were sold into slavery—some in the West Indies, and some to the Saracens in North Africa. It is to be remembered that in this country we had a very difficult time in obtaining any episcopate—not so much because of the reluctance of our Mother Church, but, rather, because of the massed opposition of the local people to the coming of any bishop. To our enemies, as well as our friends, a bishop stands for something.

Our Church is profoundly conscious of the fact that the bishop is the only continuing pastor. It is also characteristic of us that we think of the Church as a family, rather than as a kingdom, or a hierarchy. We Anglicans do not do well in thinking in terms of hierarchy; that is not our genius. If one wishes hierarchical thinking, the Roman Catholic Church will do it, and do it with great integrity, and great intelligence—it is the Roman genius. This is not our genius, nor is it our way.

Our people are profoundly *Episcopalian*. They love their bishop. They do not think of their bishop, first and foremost, as a great prince. They do not think of him in terms of being a prince at all. Rather, they think of him in terms of being their own pastor—the one to whom they can go as their Father-in-God. It is for this reason that Confirmation matters so terribly to our Church.

The word *confirmation* derives remotely from the Latin verb *confirmo*. *Confirmo*, in classical Latin, means "to strengthen the courage to be." There is almost no finer word in existence. "To strengthen the courage to be"—that is what Confirmation is all about.

We are people with a history. Israel is our mother, and we are the continuation of that Israel. The practice of the Laying on of Hands derives of course from the practice of ancient Israel. The physical act of laying on hands—that which the Hebrew describes as *s'amakh*, which means to "rest the hand upon"—was the regular form for transferring responsibility. In ancient religion, this meant responsibility for any action, whether the action be evil or good. This always comes to us as a shock, but one could find in Israel the "scapegoat"—it is a phrase we know, but how rarely do we remember what it means. It means that an animal is especially chosen, and by laying hands on the animal the sin of the people is transferred to the animal, and the animal goes away and takes away with it the people's sin. In the same way, the power of prophecy was conveyed by the laying on of hands. This is a desperately important point. The prophets laid hands on their successors, and the very laying on of hands was the outward and visible expression of the internal gift which God had already revealed to be his will. With that honesty characteristic of Israel, a prophet could not assume that his successor was going to be all that he hoped for. It was not that easy. This is illustrated by the scene between Elijah and Elisha. Elijah knows that now the time has come for him to go, but Elisha just follows along after him, as he moves from place to place—with excuse after excuse to get there. He does not wish to die in the face of his successor. He asks, in the process of getting there, if there is anything that he can do for Elisha, and Elisha asks for a double portion of Elijah's spirit. Elijah can't give him that; possibly it is something which is left entirely up to God. Elijah has made him a prophet because God revealed the vocation, but he can't guarantee this double portion of his spirit. Only if Elisha can see him when the *shekinah*— the fiery splendor of God—comes to absorb him, will the double portion come. Elisha does see him, and the double portion falls on him. This is complete spiritual honesty.

The ordination of elders in Israel was done invariably by the laying on of hands. The ordinary religion of the Hebrew, apart from the Temple, the religion of his daily life, was one very largely dominated by laymen. It had many things in common with old-fashioned New England Congregationalism. In strict theory, under congregational polity, the elders of the congregation can make an agreement with the minister as to the faith he shall preach, and as to the ministry he shall do, and how he shall do it. In a strict sense, this is true of a synagogue nowadays. The head of a synagogue is not the Rabbi, but the President of the Congregation. He is the chief elder. This body of elders is a body of advice, but with spiritual powers. In exact terms it is a collegium— the collection together of mature, godly men. This idea, both as a body and as a principle, comes over into the Christian ministry. The first ministers, in our sense of the word, were bishops and deacons. The elders continued to be the college of advice, the godly substance of a parish, and the godly strength of a diocese. It is only later, when the bishop can no longer be everywhere to celebrate, because of the spread of Christianity and the large areas to be covered, that he asks this college to take over part of his pastoral responsibility to his people.

In our Lord's own life, his baptism was followed by what one would have to call the reception of the Spirit. Whenever we use the words "the reception of the Spirit," however, we are already in danger, because the Western mind so easily thinks of the Holy Ghost as some kind of divine reservoir of spiritual balm which is given out in small or large editions. This is unfortunate. Often in the training of very bright children there comes the awful problem for the child as to the necessity of Confirmation. The child was made a member of the Church at Baptism, he received the Holy Ghost at Baptism, and the curious impression the child now has is that the Church at Baptism really had its fingers crossed, and didn't give all the things it said it was going to give, and so is keeping these as a sort of extra dividend which comes with Confirmation.

Yet, in sound theology, the Holy Spirit is nothing less

than the Life-Giver; the very reason I can write, the very reason you can read, the very reason we exist as persons, is because of the Holy Spirit. This is the Spirit which God breathes into his creation (the Hebrew and Greek words used imply that the Holy Spirit is like wind or breath); he is really the breath of God. This is the true breath by which all creatures live. Thus, when Jesus goes to his baptism, it is the Spirit which leads him to it. When Jesus is baptized, there is the Spirit expressed. And we must not assume that the chronology of his understanding has to do with divisions in the gift of the Grace of the Holy Ghost. It is in coming up from the waters of baptism that our Lord knows who he is. (In that exquisite insight in the Eastern Church this is the *first* great Epiphany; it is the "manifestation" of Christ to himself.) His baptism and understanding of the gift of the Spirit left a tremendous impression both on our Lord and on all teaching contained in the Synoptic Gospels.

At the Feast of Pentecost, the ancient feast of the Law, St. Luke tells of the Apostles being together in one place and being of one mind—an essential part. The gift of the Spirit is on the Feast of the Law, which is, in liturgical and chronological sequence, exactly the point of St. Paul's theology. (St. Luke is St. Paul's disciple!) In reading the account in Acts, it is best that it be read at the top of the lungs and just as fast as is humanly possible; then one senses the tremendous power of the sheer pouring forth of the richness of the Spirit. This is what our God is like! It has the explosive, enthusiastic quality which marked the early Church.

The Spirit is given at Pentecost, however, *without* any laying on of hands; no human agency is involved. There is also mentioned a form appropriate to the Gentiles, where also the Spirit is given before baptism. It is, for the Gentiles, their form of Pentecost.

While Peter yet spake these words, the Holy Ghost fell on all them which heard the word. And they of the circumcision which believed were astonished, as many as came with Peter, because that on the Gentiles also was poured out the gift of the Holy Ghost. For they heard them speak with tongues, and magnify God. Then answered Peter, Can any man forbid water, that these should not be baptized, which have received the Holy Ghost as well as we? And he commanded them to be baptized in the name of the Lord. (Acts 10:44-8)

In this Gentile version of Pentecost, the Holy Spirit comes directly on his people, without any human ministration in between. Sound theology of the Holy Ghost must always be aware of this—the Holy Ghost will do as he will. This is always true. Therefore, we, who are part of the ancient Church and care terribly about our orthodoxy, must never be in the position of denying the gift of the Spirit where God himself in his own way has given that Spirit. To do so is to deny the whole theology of the Church; it is to deny specifically that marvelous insight into the mind of Christ concerning the Spirit, which is accounted in St. John's Gospel in the colloquy between Jesus and Nicodemus.

In the Johannine Epistle we find this same order preserved perfectly. The phrase, "the Spirit, the Water, and the Blood," is a liturgical phrase, and what it really means is Confirmation, Baptism, and Holy Communion—in that order! This was characteristic of the Syrian Church for a long time. It will be remembered that St. Paul had his conversion, a gift of the Spirit, without human intervention.

In all his Epistles, he makes it perfectly clear that this gift was direct. When Ananias lays his hands upon Saul of Tarsus and baptizes him, he is but recognizing an action which God has already taken.

The general apostolic practice was to have Baptism followed by Confirmation, but it is to be noted that, in the early Church, the sequence was not important. The important thing is that in Baptism a person is placed in an atmosphere and a context where Christianity is possible, and it is done by the free act of a loving Father. In Confirmation is given maturity and joy in the spirit of God. It is the special gift which God gives for any special job at any special time to any person anywhere. This is its strength and its power.

In the Epistle to the Hebrews, we have the account of Baptism and the Laying on of Hands as now having come to be regarded as essential, so that one finds the phrase "of the doctrines of baptisms, and of laying on of hands, and of resurrection of the dead, and of eternal judgment." (Hebrews 6:2) These were the things which, by that time, the Church required as the very articles of the Christian faith. Baptism, the Laying on of Hands, the Resurrection of the Dead, and Eternal Judgment are still the core of Christianity. We go on to II Timothy and find that it is of critical importance because it seems to equate the Laying on of Hands with some generalized Christian ministry, quite apart from the gift of the Spirit for a specific work within the Church.

The ease with which Confirmation is made analogous to other situations is always somewhat confusing. One popular phrase describes Confirmation as "the Ordination to the status of laity within the Church." It is almost right, but the real trouble is Baptism does just that. The "priesthood of all believers" is common to Baptism; it is not some special thing held out and given at the time of Confirmation. With our Anglican passion for maturity, we tend to use the analogy of the state. We point out that whereas a child grows up as a citizen, it is still only at a specific age that the child can be accounted a man or woman and be enabled to take on the voting privileges and obligations of mature citizenship. It isn't quite that easy either, however, because in Baptism all the necessary gifts for maturity have been given. Maturity is not something dependent upon external hands, even the hands of the chief pastor.

Wherefore I put thee in remembrance that thou stir up the gift of God, which is in thee by the putting on of my hands. For God hath not given us the spirit of fear; but of power, and of love, and of a sound mind. (II Timothy 11:6-7)

Titus may have this same meaning.

Not by works of righteousness which we have done, but according to his mercy he saved us, by the washing of regeneration, and renewing of the Holy Ghost. (Titus 3:5)

This does not mean, by the way, making the Holy Ghost new. It means, rather, being made new in the Holy Ghost. One should note also the passage in II Corinthians:

Now he which stablisheth us with you in Christ, and hath anointed us, is God . . . (II Corinthians 1:21)

and that in St. John's First Epistle:

But have an unction from the Holy One and ye know all things. . . . But the anointing which ye have received of him abideth in you, and ye need not that any man teach you: but as the same anointing teacheth you of all things, and is truth and is no lie, and even as it hath taught you, ye shall abide in him. (I John 2:20, 27)

Whether this implies that anointing, the actual use of oil, was associated with Confirmation in that day, we do not know. Anointing was so common a practice in Israel (anointing for every office), and as a daily practice in ordinary Greek life, that we really do not know whether this phrase is used figuratively or not. In either case, it is not important. The use of anointing in Israel was for the making of prophets, priests, and kings. This may strengthen the argument for anointing, but the real point is that it is prayer and the laying on of hands by the chief pastor which does it. This is the covenanted arrangement by which the Lord hath bound us.

I would remind you that one of the sternest Churchmen in the history of the Church once remarked to a man: "We may not bind others by the same rules with which God has bound us." [1] That is perfect charity. We are bound by these rules, but we may not bind others by them. Here is a quotation from the great John Cosin, and is characteristic of Anglican piety.

Therefore the ancient Fathers and Bishops of the Church everywhere in their learned, Godly, and Christian writing impute unto it those gifts and graces of the Holy Ghost, which doth not make men and women Christians, as they were at first in their baptism, but, when they are made such there, assisteth them in all virtue and armeth them the better against all the several temptations of the world and the devil, to resist the wiles of the flesh.[2]

This is a perfectly sound theory.

In our whole practice as to the age of Confirmation, we must remember that in the West the problem was *maturity*. For example, in medieval times Confirmation was administered at the time when a boy went to work. We forget that a boy went to work at a very early age, that he was married at a very early age. In our day we talk about early marriage, yet we don't really know anything about early marriages! Shakespeare writes of Juliet as being fourteen, and that was fairly late. Ordinarily, it was at eleven and twelve. The Hebrew law for the age of giving a woman in marriage was twelve! Therefore, when a boy was at the point of taking on his life work, this was the time when the Church confirmed him. Gradually the age changes as civilization gets a little more thoughtful of the young. Schooling is lengthened, men and women start to work later; and as this goes on, Confirmation is put off to a later age.

About this whole matter of age there is a very serious problem. We, with our Anglo-Saxon, Northern European backgrounds tend very largely to think of responsibility in terms of mature judgment. We are quick to object: "How can you bring a child nine years old to be confirmed? The child doesn't know what it's doing." It is, of course, equally true that there are some thirty-year-olds who don't know any better what they are doing. The notion that a child, as being mature for its own age, is incapable of understanding the action of God is an unwarranted assumption. We may for other reasons decide that this is not the best age, but we have to be perfectly honest about it. We must not forget that there are people such as George Herbert, one of the holiest men in the history of our Communion, who was confirmed as a very young child; yet nobody really would say that he had not taken in the point of his Confirmation. Father Tribe (who, by the way, was trained in medicine before he went into Holy Orders), a most learned man, a first-class psychiatrist along with being a first-class priest, has this to say: "For a year after puberty the psychical system is so unstable that it is wise not to attempt to throw into it any new elements, but to let it carry on with the old." [3] This is a very wise observation. It has been said in other ways. This is how W. K. Lowther Clarke puts it:

The Anglican tradition of associating Confirmation with adolescence is deeply rooted. It is still defended by those who lay stress on instruction rather than on sacramental grace. But by others the wisdom of our present methods is disputed. Two among many utterances may be quoted. A distinguished psychologist writes: 'Adolescence is the period at which there is a normal increase of sexual feeling and therefore a normal increase of guilt feeling. It is the time at which priggishness is most liable to be needed psychologically as an evasion of guilt. . . . The adolescent knight is often more interested in the gorgeousness of his armour and the purity of his motive than in the distant goal of the Holy Grail and the imperilled lady. It is therefore perhaps unfortunate that this should be the time that is usually chosen for seizing upon a boy's religious enthusiasm, which is too often mixed with unconscious motives, with a view to Confirmation. . . . Confirmation at this phase of rapid growth and emotional instability will too often lead to undesirable repressions, or to a later regret and refusal of religious experience.' [4]

I should add that this has been made only too clear.

The Bishop of New York has insisted that a Commission, appointed by him, work out the whole matter of

Confirmation. The Commission was required by him first to produce a definition of Confirmation: What is it? Sentimentally, you and I are all in need of it, and we like it. Every human instinct inside us, every religious instinct inside us, makes us understand the laying on of the bishop's hands. This goes back centuries, even thousands of years, in our subconscious, and it makes perfect sense. This is the father's approval, the father's strength, the father's commission, given in the most ancient and most primitive of ways. But what does it really mean? If we really believe in Baptism as the gift of the Holy Ghost, in Baptism as making a person really a member of the Kingdom—not a little, potential member, but actually a child of God and an inheritor of the Kingdom—then what does Confirmation mean? Is it really just a charming ceremony? If it is, we should be sufficiently iconoclast to want it done away with. We had a Reformation once to get rid of a whole number of charming ceremonies, and we should be perfectly willing to have another Reformation at any time. Useless ceremonial is in its own way near to being the utmost blasphemy. Confirmation does matter, for it is part and parcel of our life.

This is the definition which the Commission adopted. Every single word in it is what, in popular jargon, is called a "loaded" word. It is the unanimous report of a Commission representative of the whole Diocese, and this is important. This is the definition:

Confirmation is God's gift, to members of Christ's Body, of the particular grace of the Holy Spirit which has been revealed, through the Apostles and the continuous experience of the Church, as being normally necessary to full sacramental life. In the Anglican Communion this gift is ministered by the Bishop, through prayer and the laying on of hands, to those believed ready to assume responsible participation in the worship and work of the holy Catholic Church.[5]

The individual phrases deserve attention:

"Confirmation is *God's gift* . . ."

> God's gift of the particular grace of the Holy Spirit is the undeserved love and present help which he offers us in the free gift of himself.

". . . to *members of Christ's Body* . . ."

> In the use of this phrase the Commission means membership as defined and accomplished by the Office of Holy Baptism.
>
> "Seeing now, dearly beloved brethren, that this child (*this person*) is regenerate, and grafted into the body of Christ's Church, let us give thanks . . ."
> and also:
> "We yield thee hearty thanks most merciful Father, that it hath pleased thee to regenerate this child (*this thy servant*) with thy Holy Spirit, to receive him for thine own child, and to incorporate him into thy holy Church."

". . . of the *particular grace* . . ."

> The particular grace of the Holy Spirit is that stirring up of the manifold gifts of the life-giver, whereby God, in a particular place and circumstance, strengthens man for the work and worship of his Church.

". . . which has been revealed, through the Apostles and the continuous experience of the Church, as being *normally necessary* . . ."

> In contradistinction to the two dominical sacraments described as "generally necessary" to salvation, Confirmation, as a Rite, is described as "normally necessary," since it of necessity presupposes the availability of the episcopate for its administration—a situation characteristic of the Church's basic norm.

". . . In the Anglican Communion this gift is ministered by the Bishop, through prayer and the laying on of hands, to those believed *ready* . . ."

Readiness involves three basic elements: desire, understanding and allegiance.

Desire includes all the motives behind the original request for Confirmation. Motives will vary but they are important because they offer a starting point for preparation.

Understanding requires both the comprehension and appreciation of the meaning of Confirmation and the nature and teaching of the Church.

Allegiance is the ultimate goal of preparation for Confirmation, for what the candidate really brings to this occasion of God's action is a declaration of love, faith and loyalty to God and to his Church. It is to be expected that this allegiance will be deepened and renewed by constant participation in the life and nurture of the Church.

". . . ready to assume *responsible* . . ."

Responsible is here used in the exact sense of the two words which make it up, "response" and "able," and emphasizes that participation in the Church has not only the nature of response to what God has already done, but that this response is sought and expected in accordance with the talents and abilities God has already given.

I should point out that this argument and thinking will stand up against any exception one may wish to bring, including the heartbreaking, touching one of the backward child—the child who is never going to be bright, the child who is never going to grow up mentally. The definition still applies, for it expects response "in accordance with the talents and abilities God has already given." If this backward child knows enough to know that he is loved, this is all the response God requires of that child.

". . . ready to assume responsible *participation* . . ."

Willed involvement in the costly and rewarding relationship with both God and men, which result from understanding and commitment.

". . . in the *worship and work* . . ."

Worship, in the context of this definition, refers to the corporate response of Christians to God as he is revealed in all creation, and supremely in Jesus Christ, understanding by this that whether it be an individual involved in his own necessary devotions, or a congregation involved in the liturgical worship required of all Churchmen, the worship is that of the whole Church.

Work: The work of the Church, in terms of this definition, is action undertaken with a sense of vocation on behalf of the Kingdom of God, and resulting from the Church's worship.

". . . the *holy Catholic Church.*"

The holy Catholic Church is the fellowship of all who believe in Jesus Christ as Lord and Saviour, and have been baptized into the Name of the Holy Trinity. This fellowship was begun by God's own act, in and through his eternal Word, and its life is continued by the power of the Holy Spirit. In this world it is manifested most completely in an outward and visible society which maintains the faith revealed in Holy Scripture, stated in the Creeds, and practiced in the sacraments, under an episcopate in succession from the Apostles.

Remember, your Bishop's real authority is not that of being *lord* over God's heritage, but that of being *Christ's heart for Christ's people*—the president of the Holy Mysteries.

II. ৰ

God's Holy Communion
with His People

CYRIL C. RICHARDSON:

The Heavenly Banquet ઌ 4.

In the New Testament church the primary note of the Lord's Supper was joy. This contrasts with the sombre character of so many of our celebrations of the Liturgy, in which the suffering of the Divine Victim has over-shadowed the primitive gladness in the Resurrection and in the joyful feasting with and on the Risen Lord in the heavenly banquet.

This theme is forcibly brought to our attention in the description of the Liturgy in Acts 2:46. "And day by day, attending the temple together and breaking bread in their homes, they partook of food with glad and generous hearts." The earliest Christians in Jerusalem still continued their attendance at the Temple and synagogue services; but they added to these the most distinctive rite of the Church— the heavenly banquet. The "breaking bread" is a technical term for the Lord's Supper which was held in different homes before there were any churches. The celebration was marked by "gladness"—indeed, the Greek word is a very emphatic one and might well be rendered "with ecstatic joy."

Wherein lay this joy? First and foremost, it was the joy of the presence of the Risen Christ. He who had been crucified was now among his disciples as they ate and drank together. We may note that several resurrection stories bring out this close association of the Risen Lord with the sacrament. In Luke 24:35 the Emmaus story concludes with the pregnant verse, "He was known to them in the breaking of bread." Other references of a similar character are to be found in Acts 10:41; John 21; and in the Church Father, Ignatius of Antioch, who in his letter to the Smyrnaeans (3:3) refers to the tradition of the appearance to Peter and its similar liturgical setting. Moreover, there is the verse in Revelation 3:20, "Behold, I stand at the door and knock." This familiar verse, too, is eucharistic, for it continues, "if any one hears my voice and opens the door, I will come in to him and eat with him, and he with me." To think of the presence of the Risen Christ was almost automatically to think of him as made known in the Liturgy where the disciple could eat and drink with him as in the days of his flesh.

This joyful note runs through the Eastern Church's interpretation of the Lord's Supper, with its emphasis on immortality and resurrection. Indeed, the consecration of the bread and wine at the time of the Epiclesis is understood as the resurrection of Christ. Appropriately, the deacon says after the Communion in the Liturgy of St. Chrysostom, "Having seen Christ's resurrection, let us adore the holy Lord Jesus Christ." The mystery of the Lord's

Supper is above all the mystery of his risen presence with his faithful Church.

It is not accidental, therefore, that the day especially chosen for the observance of the Liturgy was Sunday, the day of the Lord's resurrection. This is early attested in the New Testament (Acts 20:7). Each week was, as it were, a celebration of Easter. The fasts of Wednesday and Friday (which are as early as the first century) commemorated the betrayal and crucifixion, while Sunday was the climax in resurrection.

The Lord's Supper, however, was not only the feast with the Risen Lord: it was a very special feast, bringing to fulfillment the hopes of Israel. It was the heavenly banquet, in which God's Kingdom, long expected, was *now* made present in a moment of time. The Messiah *had* come; Israel's hopes *had* been fulfilled; the reality of the heavenly world *had* now broken into our time. This theme we are accustomed to designate by the term "realized eschatology"—an unnecessarily bewildering phrase for what every Christian confesses—namely, that God's Kingdom is now present, and especially in the Liturgy. Here God's purposes are being fulfilled; here his grace is poured out abundantly; here the heavenly realm breaks in upon our earthly existence. Heaven is not a place far off, to be awaited by the Christian and only entered on death. Heaven is now, in every moment when God's triumphant glory is manifest in the victory of Christ. In the Liturgy we are in heaven, as with the saints and angels we feast at the celestial banquet and enter into the fulfillment of Israel's expectations. This idea is well indicated in a motto to be seen in the dome of many Greek churches: "Standing in the temple of his glory, we think we stand in heaven."

One of the ways in which Judaism pictured the end of the ages when God's purposes would be fulfilled and his salvation vindicated was by a heavenly feast. There are several references to this in sayings of Jesus (Matthew 8:11; Luke 14:15; 22:30), and this is the meaning of "Abraham's bosom" in the story of Dives and Lazarus. The latter lies in Abraham's bosom—that is, at the place of honor in the heavenly banquet, it being the ancient custom to dine reclining. For other references to this picture of the heavenly banquet see Zechariah 8:19; and, in the later Jewish literature, Enoch 62:14; Baruch 29:30. Jewish apocalyptic developed this theme extensively.[1] It was imagined that God would provide a great feast at the end of the ages for his faithful. The Messiah would come from heaven, bringing with him the celestial food of "manna," which the children of Israel had eaten in the wilderness and which had been ground in one of the seven heavens.

It is this imagery which the earliest Christians applied to the Lord's Supper. It was the heavenly banquet in which the end of the ages was already manifest and God's victory already accomplished. To eat and drink at the Lord's Table was to enter into the fulfillment of Israel's hope. Thus it is that John's Gospel understands the Lord's Supper in terms of the manna come down from heaven (6:31-32). Christ himself is the manna of the heavenly banquet. Another way in which this symbolism was developed was in terms of the sacred fish, by which the Eucharist is often represented in catacomb painting, and which is perhaps implied in the stories of the feedings of the multitudes, as well as in Luke 24:42 and John 21:13. The sacred fish is the main course at the heavenly banquet in Jewish apocalyptic, although the symbol has many other meanings.[2]

The joy of the Lord's Supper is thus the joy of the presence of the Risen Christ, and of participation in God's victory which even now we can experience. But there was in early Christianity a full realization that, while we have a foretaste of the Kingdom, we do not yet enjoy the consummation. The Church stands in the interim between the victory won in Christ and that final fulfillment when there will be a new heaven and a new earth. There is always a "not yet" to be put beside the "now." There is ever a tension between the victory won and the victory to be appropriated. Hence the Liturgy, while never detracting from the way in which the Kingdom *is* now manifest in the Risen Christ, looks also beyond this present to the consummation which is not yet. The "Advent" theme is there along with the theme of fulfillment. By "Advent" the early Church meant the coming of Christ when sin would be fully destroyed and God be "all in all." So Paul in I Corinthians 11:26 speaks of the celebration of the Supper as proclaiming the Lord's death "until he comes"; and a typical liturgical cry of the ancient Church, preserved from earliest times in its Aramaic form was *Maranatha*—"Lord come"! (*Didache* 10:6.) The Supper was proclamation of God's mystery of salvation now made present, but looking, too, to its consummation when God's glory would be everywhere manifest.

In the joyful theme of the Supper which we have indicated, there did, of course, lie dangers. It was easy to pass from gladness to license; and that is indeed what happened in Corinth. What Paul had to face in that all too human congregation was joy run riot. It would appear that the Christians there met together to have a feast which had deteriorated into a church supper beset with cliques and in which physical enjoyment was overshadowing the spiritual ends of the meal. The rich would not share their picnic baskets with the poor: each went ahead with his own meal without waiting for others, and Christian fellowship was disrupted by license and selfishness. So it is that Paul recalls the Corinthians to the proper purpose of the Supper. It is to manifest true fellowship by participating in the mystery of the death of Christ. This solemn note in Paul is a purposeful attempt to offset the evils which had fallen upon the Corinthian observance of the Liturgy, and is a necessary corrective to the dangers in the more primitive emphasis on joy and gladness. But we should be wrong to neglect this more primitive note. All too long our celebrations of the Liturgy have moved within the sombre context of the medieval Western Church. We need, while never forgetting the basic theme of the Divine Victim with which we shall deal in a later chapter, to recover the thrilling gladness of the Lord's Supper. Here we eat and drink with the Risen Christ and partake of the banquet of the end of the ages. Here we know that all God's promises have found their "yes" in Christ (II Corinthians 1:20), and that is why we say the *Amen* in the Liturgy, affirming the victory already ours. For *Amen* does not look to future fulfillment only, "So be it"; but it is the Christian confession, "So it *is*," even now in the work accomplished by Christ, who is both host and food in the heavenly banquet.

We may conclude by trying to picture a celebration

of the Supper in Jerusalem in the earliest days of the Church. We should imagine a two-story house with an outside staircase. On a Sunday, about sundown, the Christians begin to gather. Each has brought a "picnic" basket of contributions to the common meal; and it is from this custom that the collection will eventually develop in the Liturgy. The guests greet each other with the usual oriental greeting of the kiss (cf. Luke 7:45), and from this the liturgical *Pax* will later enter the service. The donations are taken upstairs to the dining room, though the guests will sit around the floor or on stools downstairs while the company is gathering. Some *hors d'oeuvres* will be served here. When all have come, they will go upstairs for the meal proper. A long table is placed down the center of the "upper room," and trestle benches with mattresses for reclining will be put around three sides of it. The meal will open with the host (an apostle, perhaps,) taking a loaf of bread and giving thanks to God for it. He will say, "Blessed art thou, O Lord our God, King of the Universe, who bringeth forth bread from the earth." This is the typical Jewish way of saying grace (preserved even today), and is accompanied by distributing pieces of the loaf to each of the guests. It was evidently in connection with this ritual act of saying grace that Jesus gave the bread its sacramental meaning at the Last Supper; and the host will doubtless add some appropriate word to this effect as he distributes the loaf. The meal will follow. Then, since the guests have been eating with their fingers, there will follow the washing of hands. A bowl and towel will be presented to each guest and from this will come the *Lavabo* in the later Liturgy. Grace after meals will now be said. The host will take a cup of wine and begin a dialogue with the guests. v. "Let us say grace." ʀ. "Blessed be the name of the Lord," etc., from which the *Sursum Corda* will later develop. The grace itself will consist of thanksgivings to God for the land, the food and the people, though these typically Jewish themes came early to be given a Christian meaning, the heavenly land, the people of the Church, and the sacramental food. Finally will come the wine blessing, "Blessed art Thou, O Lord our God, King of the Universe, who createst the fruit of the vine." As with the bread, so it was in connection with the blessing or grace after meals that Jesus gave the wine its sacramental meaning; and the host will add some words to this effect. The cup will then be circulated among the guests. The evening will conclude with psalm singing, prophesying, exhortation, and the singing perhaps of some new Christian hymns, fragments of which (in their Greek form) have been preserved in the New Testament (cf. Ephesians 5:14; Revelation 5:9; 5:12-13; 12:10-12; 19:1-2; 19:6). The note of joy in the presence of the Risen Christ will be evident throughout. These disciples know they have tasted of the powers of the age to come and been partakers of the Messianic Banquet.

EDWARD N. WEST:

The Knowledge
of the Risen Lord ❧   5.

In the fourth chapter of Genesis we encounter one of those extraordinary stories which makes almost no sense in terms of its setting. "And she bare Cain. And she again bare his brother Abel. And Abel was a keeper of sheep, but Cain was a tiller of the ground. And in process of time it came to pass, that Cain brought of the fruit of the ground an offering unto the Lord. And Abel, he also brought of the firstlings of his flock and of the fat thereof. And the Lord had respect unto Abel and to his offering: but unto Cain and to his offering he had not respect." (Genesis 4:1-5)

Anyone who has taught children is aware of the problem in trying to account as to why the Lord accepted Abel's sacrifice and not Cain's. I regret to say that most of the clergy, being quite smart in defeating small fry, resort to this approach: "Well, obviously if you look at Cain's nature, you will discover why the Lord, knowing what his nature was like, didn't accept his offering. Cain, after all, killed his brother and, if he was that kind of person, you can understand why God didn't accept his offering." It is a nice piece of back-reading, but it is not quite all that there is to be said on the subject. We must remember that in great portions of the Old Testament there are vestigial remains of the tremendous battle between the nomad desert people and those settled in communities—the agrarian or the city people. The nomad people did not like the city people; they did not trust them. They did not like the people of the land, the tillers of the soil; they did not trust them either. They thought that soft and easy living made for immorality; they had all the evidence of the city to gaze upon, and everything they saw bore out their judgment. If one wishes to understand a man such as the Prophet Amos, one must understand that he is a harsh, desert nomad, with the fierce morality of his kind, coming in and seeing sights which no one ever should see, and, having seen them, being overcome with rage against these things, seeing nothing but God's anger weighing over the city people and the settled lands. Everything was rotten, ready to fall off the vine; it was all so bad, so regrettable.

In order for us to understand this with some intelligence, we must remember that sacrifice, in its ordinary sense, is just as ancient as religion itself. There had always been the killing of animals in order to appease a god or to avert some kind of trouble, but there had been another form of animal killing which was connected with totems. *Totemism* is a word which has been derived recently in liturgics through an understanding of the religions of people who use totem poles. There is always in totemism a belief in a divine tribal ancestor who has an agreed-upon animal or bird—a sacred representation—which, under certain circumstances, if killed, produces a (very primitive) form of communion between the divine tribal ancestor and the people. And it is not only communion between the ancestor and the people, but it is communion within the tribe itself. This is how people know each other to belong to this particular tribe.

The Semites, the sons of Shem, which included, of course, the Hebrews, the Arabs, and the Ethiopians, held to this form of animal sacrifice. Israel was remarkable in that it held to this form of totemism, so that instead of offering an animal just to avert the anger of a petty local god, it offered this animal in a profound conviction that God was the father of Israel and that God, through this animal, had communion with his people and the people had communion one with another. This particular form of sacrifice in Israel was known as the *Pesach*. This was the sacrifice which was held in the spring. It, of course, had to do with the hope that the flocks would be fertile, but it also had to do with the notion that, by communion with God, the people themselves were fulfilling their own appointed destiny.

Please remember that this is a twentieth-century way of describing a very simple and straightforward piece of religion. The native peoples of the land, particularly of the land that Israel eventually went into, Philistia (from which we have Palestine), and of the land of Canaan, had a feast which came about the same time, but it was a feast of unleavened bread—*Mazzoth* (from which is derived the word which we now know as *matzos*), and this feast of

Mazzoth was despised by the nomad people! It is over and against such a dislike that we find the setting of the story of Cain and Abel. Cain is offering the Mazzoth; Abel is offering the Pesach. One represents the offering of the land, and the other represents the offering which is related to the divine tribal god. Read that way, one can see why, of necessity, Cain's sacrifice would be unacceptable to any (Hebrew) God. We do not read Scripture as the Hebrew read it, because we read it out of context. He read it with all the fierce power of his nomad religion behind him.

When the Israelites were in Egypt (if we take the account in the Old Testament exactly as it stands), Moses asked for permission to take his people for a three-day journey into the wilderness to sacrifice to their god. This is, of course, the Pesach—the spring sacrifice to God— far more ancient than any journey into or out of Egypt. The ultimate connection between this Pesach and the Passover is a reading-back into the original situation. Moses wanted to take his people out into the wilderness to sacrifice to their god. Totemism? Of course, naturally it is, but on top of all this totemism is laid the evidence of God's almighty hand in the delivery of his people from Egypt.

The sheer number of references and ideas included makes the transition difficult to follow. Passover, which has come to mean the idea that the Angel of Death passed over the houses of the Israelites, because the Israelites had now already put the blood of the lamb on the door lintel, also marks the delivery of Israel at the Red Sea. It has all become God's mighty delivery of his people.

They arrived in Philistia, and there encountered at first

hand the religion of the land. The exact dating of the Passover by the feast of unleavened bread through an apparently natural process of history is quite understandable. It is not as easy to account for the use of bread, a product of the land! In this connection we must notice that terribly important and most mysterious figure of the Old Testament, though mentioned rarely, Melchizedek. *Melchizedek*—the word in Hebrew means the king, or righteous one—is the priest-king of Salem. Salem, as used in the early portion of Genesis, was an indeterminate kind of place, although its connection with peace is clear from the word *Shalom*. When Melchizedek is referred to in the Psalms, *Salem* certainly stands for the holy city, Jerusalem. This priest-king came to Abraham, when his name was still Abram, and offered him *bread* and wine. This is bread within a genuinely religious context.

One can see why the Fathers of the early Church were so taken by the "type" of Melchizedek—a priest-forever of whom there is neither an account of his coming from anywhere, nor an account of his dying. Yet this totally different kind of man was acknowledged by Israel to be a priest of the most high God, a royal priest who could bless even the patriarch of Israel. Rabbinic thinking is not as squeamish and as delicate as ours tends to be. By blessing Abraham, Melchizedek had blessed the seed which was already in Abraham; therefore even the priesthood of Aaron had ultimately been blessed by Melchizedek. Thus he is a priest of a higher order, a priest of eternal significance.

The reference to Melchizedek in the Psalter is not quite the same thing. This reference is to justify the Maccabeans (the great people one reads of in the Apocrypha), who were not quite legitimate. They were not the "sons of David" in the strict sense. They did not have the hereditary high priesthood in the strict sense. Therefore this is used to justify a priesthood which is so transparently of God as to make physical descent of no importance. Melchizedek thus becomes the figure of a spiritual thing rather than an inherited priesthood.

It should be remembered that every person whose name is Cohen is automatically a priest. *Cohen* is the Hebrew word for priest. It is a hereditary priesthood, and therefore does not depend upon vocation, morality, ability or consecration. Even in Old Testament days, prophets were on the side of the priesthood of Melchizedek as opposed to the Aaronite priesthood. This becomes extraordinarily clear later, in the days of the great Maccabeus.

A good portion of what we know about the worship of Israel, of course, comes from post-Exilic days. We know a little about the *Mazzoth* of the land, and we know a little about the *Pesach* of the ancient people—which in their origin were just ordinary feasts of ordinary people. *Kazir*, the feast of weeks, was the end of the harvest; *Asiph* marked the in-gathering of the harvest; and *Succoth* was the feast of booths. Pain and suffering, however, leave marks on religion. Pain and suffering, in the Exile, left extraordinary marks on Israel's religion. *Succoth*, which was originally a harvest-home festival, now became the feast marking the end of the reading of the Torah. This is not what it meant in the beginning—that is quite beside the point. In religion, God uses people, ideas, and things exactly as and where they are, and then takes them and moves them on to where he wants them to be.

A pre-Exilic Israelite would not have remotely understood what a "sin offering" meant. A sin offering is something which is thought of only after the conscience of a great people is "convicted" of sin, and they stand before their god as sinners. It is no longer the "scapegoat" type of approach—in which, if something goes wrong, or some poor wretch does something he shouldn't in some place where he shouldn't, or if things are going bad, or the crops aren't coming right, or the animals are dying—then everything can be straightened out by putting the sin on some animal, and getting rid of the animal. It is very primitive, yet it is a form of religion which each of us has known at some time. It is still the religion of small children. The movement from this to the lofty prophetic notion that the sin of a people includes the suffering of any one of the people is the loftiest portion of Old Testament religion. If my brother, in the remotest part of the world, suffers, then I too, as a true son of Israel, suffer. If my brother sins, I sin. We are all a part of each other. This is a long way from the original totemism; it is a profound insight into our communion with one another. Christianity has come to see this to be almost the central feature in redemption, because our Lord took on everybody's sin and carried it away with love. This is the very core of the atonement, our at-one-ment with God.

Early religion had joy, and this was a good thing. We read the 150th Psalm, and forget that the timbrels are the strange little things which still accompany dancing in the West Indies. The phrase, "bind the sacrifice with cords to the altar," had nothing to do with binding a sacrifice at all. It meant men all joining hands and dancing around the altar. We do not think of dancing in church. When John Henry Newman talks about "the dance of the liturgy," he is really expressing nothing but a rather extraordinary bit of medievalism. The gaiety of our liturgical dancing is not quite the same as Israel's! They danced before the Ark. On the feast of Succoth, they took out the scrolls of the Law and danced with the scrolls in their arms. They had joy in their God, and this was a joy made even sharper by the price they had had to pay to still believe in God. This is not primitive religion; this is the most cultivated kind of religion. We use the Psalms which come from the hymnal of the second Temple, and if we read them through we come to the glorious "hallel" psalms, the praise-God psalms. We are not temperamentally equipped to say "Hallelujah." We are not good at it!

Israel had what you and I would term a loud-mouthed religion. However loud-mouthed, though, it had sacrifice and unendurable pain behind it! We must never underestimate the Apocrypha, in particular, the Books of the Maccabees. The period in which our Lord was incarnate was one dominated by the immediate history we read in the Apocrypha, and by some of the thinking found in the latest sections of the book ascribed to the prophet Daniel. When the writer tells of people being "torn asunder," this is not a figure of speech—they were literally "torn asunder." Some of the reading in the Apocrypha is grim beyond words: children cooked in front of their mothers in order to make their mothers deny the God of Israel; men skinned alive; men impaled; people "who left no memorial." This is the kind of atmosphere which was behind Israel's joy. It makes any other kind of joy seem fatuous. The easy joy which has never known the counsel of pain cannot mean anything in terms of serious religion.

Synagogue worship was made up of a set of lections and psalms, and, generally, preaching. The lections always included one from the Law and one from the Prophets. A synagogue had to have a fixed number of men to say the "Amen," and this is in the background of our Lord's thinking when he talks about two or three gathered together in his Name. They were agreeing with each other in saying the "Amen." For a Hebrew it is unthinkable that a man could do real liturgical religion all alone. Liturgy *means* public work, and, in particular, the public work of the people of God. It is generally conceded that our Lord's own immediate group constituted a synagogue. It was a synagogue meeting in the "upper room." It had the right number of men; it had a ruler, and all the other necessary things. It had the usual *Kiddush,* a religious meal held on the eve of a feast, at which a discourse was given. That our Lord should have a synagogue of his own was not unusual. In Israel now, and particularly in Jerusalem, these tiny synagogues still exist. For example, there will be a synagogue of Romanian people, or a synagogue of people who speak a special form of Hebrew. One finds all these little national groups. In our Lord's day there were also local political groups which met as synagogues. There was, for example, the synagogue of "the libertines." All these little groups had enough men to say the "Amen." If the emphasis seems to be on *men,* it is because Israel had a man's religion. If there were ten million women in one place and only nine men, there could not be a synagogue. A "mother in Israel" might have great dignity, but, in terms of religion and the public work of prayer, it was a man's religion. Women have become valuable to the Church, as souls and as persons, because of the incarnation of our Lord. There is no other great religion still extant in which a woman is regarded so completely as a person in her own right.

Synagogue worship started with two benedictions. *Benediction,* to Israel, meant the blessing of God for something; it did not mean blessing people or things apart from God. Were I, in Hebrew terms to bless you, I would say, "Blessed art thou O Lord our God, King Eternal, who hast planted these thy servants in thy kingdom." The blessing of bread was: "Blessed art thou O Lord, our God, King of the Universe, who bringest forth bread from the earth." The blessing of the cup was: "Blessed art thou O Lord, our God, King of the Universe, who bringest forth the fruit of the vine . . .", and twice a year was added, "which maketh glad the heart of man." In every instance it is a blessing God. At a later date, Israel started to include the *Shema,* the first word in Hebrew of the *Shema Yisroel:* "Hear O Israel, the Lord our God is one Lord, and thou shalt love the Lord thy God with all thy heart, with all thy soul, with all thy strength." This became a creedal statement for the Jews only after trouble over Christians. There is no evidence that it was used, apart from ordinary rabbinic discourse, up to the time of the struggles with Christians in the synagogues. When our Lord uses it, or when he praises it in the mouth of a lawyer, he is just agreeing with the common rabbinic tradition. The Decalogue was said in an antiphonal form, not totally unlike the old-fashioned use of the Decalogue in our communion service. Then followed, "Blessed be the Name of the glory of his kingdom," and the various prayers. There was a lesson from the Pentateuch, a lesson from the Prophets, the Aaronic blessing ("The Lord bless you and keep you"), and then a sermon. The sermon was not essential; the ruler of a synagogue asked if any man was moved by the Spirit to preach. If, of course, he recognized a man as a rabbi, as the ruler of the synagogue did when he saw our Lord standing in the middle of ten or a dozen men, he would invite him to preach. It is always a slight source of pain to realize that among the ancient Hebrews, as with the Quakers, a man did not preach unless the Spirit moved him. It may be only a base libel, but it is alleged that, in some Christian churches of the orthodox tradition, some men have on occasion preached *without* the Spirit moving them.

Synagogue worship was devised for small groups. Dr. Richardson has pointed out that the early Church's worship was in houses—private family affairs. It did not do well in big scale. Every time that the acoustics of the Cathedral Church of St. John the Divine seem slightly difficult, one remembers with comfort that in the synagogue at Alexandria the minister had to use a flag to signal the people when it was time to say "Amen." It was characteristic of Israel that men stood for prayer. In the early Church, as in Israel, the belief was that the praise of God required a man to stand on his feet. There is still something to be said for it.

What actually took place at this meeting in the Upper Room? There was, of course, the *Kiddush,* the religious meal of a rabbi and his immediate synagogue. There are the ordinary thanksgivings for bread and wine, coming actually at two ends of the meal. This is noted in the words "likewise *after supper* he took the cup." This means two ends of a meal with a regular parish-supper kind of thing right in the middle.

It is almost impossible to convey in English that which was conveyed in Aramaic by our Lord's words. English, which is a magnificent language, has certain extraordinary irrationalities, and there is one thing which cannot be said in English (unless you are Winston Churchill), but which is the only way of making our Lord's words clear. Our Lord takes bread and utters the blessing, *"Blessed art thou O Lord, our God, King Eternal, who bringest forth bread from the earth."* (His hand would be out, and, characteristically, he would be looking up, which was unusual enough for the Gospels to remark on it.) He takes the bread, breaks it, looks at them and says, "This is me." We spend so much of our life worrying about what he said in terms of this being his Body, that we tend, in our reading back, to become lost in beautiful liturgical language. What his own Hebrew friends heard him say—and *mean*—was, *"This is me!"* It is a declaration of intention for Good Friday. One does not even remotely understand Good Friday unless he realizes that all which takes place on the night before is done with the Cross in full view. The phrase "This my blood of a new covenant," or testament, becomes a little more liturgical in St. Paul's account! *"This Cup is the new covenant in my blood."* In St. Luke we find also a reference to the Messianic banquet. St. Luke is not really interested, actually, in the chalice, as are the other men. He is concerned with bread and the banquet.

It is not, however, because of Maundy Thursday, or even Good Friday, that you and I go to communion services. We do not have an annual commemoration of a fine, good, and holy man who did wonderful things in our world long ago. Israel did just that. Israel met once a year to remember the mighty act of God by which they had been delivered, and remembrance itself constituted Israel's sacrifice. We go to the Eucharist because of the experience shown forth in the magnificent account which is our Gospel for Easter Monday. Two disciples were going down to Emmaus and they were joined by a Stranger. (It is worth remembering that our Lord, in any of the Resurrection appearances, was never recognized on sight. He was recognized by Mary Magdalene only when he pronounced her name. He was recognized by others through the sight of his wounds, or by his characteristic cry of "Shalom," uttered in his own particular way.) They were just going along and they did not recognize him either. There follows a discourse on the nature of God's Messiah: What kind of Messiah had God really wanted? It is perfectly clear from the Gospel accounts that the disciples themselves were not agreed as to what form of Messiah it should be. St. Peter at one time said, "Oh, you can't go up to Jerusalem and suffer!" At that time, the Lord turned on him in anger and said, *"Get thee behind me, that talk is not of God, it is of the devil."* It is perfectly clear that poor wretched Judas thought that somehow or other he could force the Lord's hand and make him assume an earthly kingdom. The Lord would not do it. It was another misunderstanding! Peter's taking out his sword, and cutting off the servant's ear at the time of the arrest, was a complete misunderstanding of the kind of Messiah Jesus was to be. So this Stranger explains to these two poor heart-broken men that God's

Messiah had had to suffer all of these things. He goes through the Old Testament and describes, point by point, what the Suffering Servant was all about. Finally, they drew near to a tiny inn, and they pressed him to remain and eat with them. He is persuaded. At the table, he utters the blessing, takes the bread, and breaks it—and they know him in the *breaking of the bread.*

This is why we go to the communion service. We go because, according to God's own plan, the continuing Resurrection experience is knowledge of a risen, reigning, triumphant Lord—in the Breaking of Bread.

Liturgiologists are notoriously inept in trying to discover what medievalists, ancient or modern, were fighting about. Since, for the liturgiologist, the knowledge of the Risen Lord in the breaking of bread is the prime matter, what type of bread was used is simply of no importance. It is clear that the bread at the inn was not unleavened, it was just ordinary bread.

Our Lord is not known only in the action of the breaking, he is known also in the bread broken. In the very broken thing itself, the useless, helpless, insignificant crumbs, God feeds us. We can ask no more formal definition of God's presence than the understanding that, as you make your communion, you are hearing—with the deep inner hearing of the soul—*"This is me."* If you understand that, you can move on to the splendors of Paul's understanding that the Body of Christ includes an awful lot more than just its sacramental expression. The early Church did not recognize four or five different kinds of Body in Christ; it was all one Body. Not to discern the Lord's Body means to St. Paul not only failing to realize what is going on in the sacrament itself, but also failing to see the mobile human vehicle of God's holy, divine, and life-giving mysteries—your neighbor. To fail to recognize another communicant as a tabernacle of the most high God is to fail to discern the Lord's Body. That is damnation. It does not mean that one is going to be damned in the hereafter, it means that one is already damned, if he cannot see Christ in his brethren.

The Eastern Church has placed its great emphasis on the mystery revealed. Eastern Orthodox theology is interested in *who* did it and *what* happened. The Western Church, of which we are a part, has always been concerned with the sacrifice commemorated. The sacrifice commemorated is that on the Cross. When? Good Friday. What did he do? He offered himself for us. What is the point of our communions? We know him in the breaking of bread. He gave thanks; we too give our thanks. Our whole liturgy is made up of the giving of thanks, but our thanks have to include him—all that he was, all that he is, all that he is going to be in and to us.

This memorial sacrifice is regarded by all Western thinkers as essential, even as for Israel sacrifice was an essential part of religion. We are not, however, going to kill a lamb. The ancient prayers of the ancient Church refer to our service as the "unbloody sacrifice." The Lamb, slain before the foundation of the world, is shown forth in figure by thousands, or even millions, of little lambs which were killed at the Passover during the passing centuries. But this is the mighty Lamb who offers himself, once and for all; it is he who is our sacrifice.

When, during the Oblation in our communion service,

we rehearse the divine mercy shown us, we are doing as Israel did—we are making memorial of this mighty act of our God. The result of it all is that we know him. We even know each other in the Breaking of Bread.

CYRIL C. RICHARDSON:

The Holy Sacrifice 6.

From earliest times the Lord's Supper was understood by the Church as a sacrificial act. In I Corinthians 10, for instance, Paul can contrast the Christian sacred meal with the cult meals held in pagan temples; and the point of the contrast lies in their both being acts of offering to those considered to be God or gods. Moreover, the curious reversal of the usual order (bread—cup) in verse 16, is only explicable on the assumption Paul is thinking of the typical pagan oblation of wine to the host-god at the beginning of a cult meal. Sacrificial imagery was the primary way in which the ancient world thought of religion. It is not surprising, therefore, that this language should have come to play a dominant part both in understanding the work of Jesus and in interpreting the Liturgy.

It was not from the prophetic tradition of the Word alone that the significance of God's victory in Jesus was expressed. Rather did sacrificial terms provide an even deeper way to understand the work of Jesus. He was the

"Lamb of God" (John 1:29), the Passover lamb (I Corinthians 5:7), whose sacrifice on the cross had fulfilled and put an end to the ancient rituals of animal sacrifice. (This is the leading theme of the *Epistle to the Hebrews*). We may note, too, that the prophetic tradition of Israel turns naturally to sacrificial language to grasp the meaning of the Servant (Isaiah 53:10).

There are two reasons why we find it hard to appreciate fully this type of symbolism. On the one hand, we are far removed from the stark realities of slaughter, flowing of blood, the smell of burning flesh, which were familiar sights and odors to the ancient world. On the other hand, the concept of ritual sacrifice has suffered by being unduly narrowed in significance, so that it has become almost wholly centered in the idea of slaughter and destruction. This is largely due to the character of medieval Western piety, whose repressive and ascetic nature gave undue emphasis to only one of the several themes in the sacrificial act. Moreover, this in turn provoked a bitter controversy in the sixteenth century, when a sharp distinction (wholly unintelligible to the ancient Church) arose between "altar" and "table"; and the understanding of the Liturgy suffered from overemphasis by both Romanists and Reformers alike. One side claimed the essence of the Lord's Supper lay in its being a veritable act of the slaughter of Christ by the priest; the other side contended it was only a remembering of the passion of Christ on Calvary. The fruitlessness of much of this controversy lay in the narrow view of sacrifice which both sides held. The full appreciation both of the symbolism of Jesus as Lamb of God and of the Liturgy as a ritual sacrifice can only be gained by a deeper and broader understanding of sacrifice itself.

What, then, is "sacrifice"? The word in Latin means "making holy" (from *sacer* and *facio*). Sacrifice is a ritual act which makes holy, which provides the means whereby man can recover his "wholeness," his "salvation." These words "whole," "holy" and "healthful" or "hale" are all related to a single Anglo-Saxon root *hāl*, which means "sound, healthy, complete." (The similar Greek root *sōs*, which means the same thing, lies behind such words as "Saviour," "salvation.") Sacrifice, then, is the act whereby man recovers his true ground in God, his Creator; whereby he comes into God's holy presence to find his own wholeness or completeness, and to overcome the disruption of his nature by sin.

How is this done? For the Christian, of course, it is done in Christ—by entering into his sufferings and the victory of his resurrection. But we shall gain new light on this if we look for a moment at ancient animal sacrifice, and see the way in which it foreshadowed the saving act of Christ and provided a fitting imagery for expressing its meaning.

Animal sacrifice belongs essentially to a nomadic economy where wealth lies in the herds and flocks one possesses. The first act in sacrifice is the choosing of the best of one's flock in order to render it to God. It is the unblemished lamb, the perfect example, which is the fitting gift. It is perhaps true that originally such a gift was made to appease the wrath of God, quite naïvely understood. At its deepest, however, the sacrificial act far surpassed such primitive views, and we are probably wrong in imagining that sacrifice had its origin wholly in making a gift to God. The significance of the communion feast on the animal and the release of vital powers by death (which we shall consider in a moment) must be taken fully into account.

To choose the most costly of one's possessions in order to render it to God is an act of great importance. It dramatically indicates the freedom of man from his possessions. By willingness to surrender what is most costly, man declares *he* possesses his possessions, they do not possess *him*. Only when we thus declare our independence of what we have and owe to God, can we rightly use it. Otherwise, we are slaves to our possessions.

Having chosen the unblemished lamb, the devotee now lays his hands on it—an act of deep mystical significance. By this he identifies himself with the animal, so that what happens to the animal he understands as happening to him. This mystical identification or participation is basic to all religious symbolism. It is a way of "acting out" the inner drama of the soul. The exterior symbols evoke emotions and acts of will which are more difficult to elicit without the external drama.

There follows the death of the animal. In the animal's death the self of the devotee dies. Not only is his richest possession given to God, but his very *self*. What happens to the animal, as we have suggested, happens to him. And then out of this dying of the self, new life emerges. That is the perpetual mystery of religious self-offering: by giving ourselves away, we gain our true selves. This is symbolized in different ways in various sacrifices of the Old Testament. Some, as the *zevach,* were divided between the worshipper and God. Thus the new life of self-offering was pictured as a mutual feast with God. Others, as the *olah,* were totally surrendered to God in the whole burnt-offering. Here the image suggested that man and all his possessions were ultimately God's, for him to do with as he pleased. But in this total surrender man found his wholeness and over-came the anxiety of his existence. Yet other sacrifices, as the passover, were wholly consumed by the worshipper. Here the animal's vital power, released by death, was understood as the new life flowing from the act of surrender.

Sacrifice was thus a dramatic way of picturing and evoking the soul's journey of salvation. Offering, dying, rising are its three basic themes; and it is these which are seen fulfilled in Christ. What the ancient ritual act only foreshadowed was victoriously achieved in him. Thus the Christian sacrifice is that in which we enter into the act of Christ, reliving in the Liturgy the offering, dying, and rising of Christ, and so participating in the salvation he accomplished. Here is the final sacrifice, bringing to an end the ancient ritual act because he has done what animal sacrifice could only hint at and suggest. By mystical identification with Christ, we, too, offer ourselves, die, and rise, and so perform the act of "making holy."

In the light of all this, it must at once become apparent how fruitless is all talk about "altar" in contrast to "table." An altar *is* a table, and a table *is* an altar. Indeed, in many languages the words are identical. An "altar" means literally a "high-table" (*altare*)—a special table on which we present our offerings to God. Since the culmination of sacrifice is a banquet, signifying the new life with God through offering and dying, there can be no distinction between table and altar. Sacrifice is table communion with God.

To illustrate this theme let us look at a series of paintings in the Roman catacombs which portray the significance of the Lord's Supper. They are found in the so-called "Crypts of the Sacraments" in the catacomb of St. Callixtus and date from the third century. They give us a very clear picture of the ancient Church's sense of the holy sacrifice. First we see a three-legged table on which lies the Eucharist (symbolized by the loaf of bread and the sacred fish). Beside the table is the bishop blessing the offering, and at the other side stands a woman in prayer. She prays with hands outstretched in the form of the cross (a Christian understanding of the ancient Roman gesture of prayer). She represents the Church, though since these pictures are in a cemetery she also signifies the soul of the deceased. The Eucharist is not bounded by space or time, but as the heavenly sacrifice it unites in one fellowship the living and dead. In this picture, then, we see the Liturgy as the offering of Christ and of the Christian.

This general picture of the Liturgy is now further explained by other frescoes. We see Abraham sacrificing Isaac. Here the theme of the Divine Victim comes to the fore. Without death new life cannot come. Isaac is both the Christ who suffers for the sin of the world, and also the Christian who enters into the dying of his Lord. Then we see a fresco of the raising of Lazarus. Here the resurrection theme is portrayed. Out of the death comes the new life; and by the dying of the self to God, the act of "making holy" is possible. Finally, we see seven men reclining at a banquet. Here is the consummation of the sacrificial act. This is the heavenly banquet. The feast in and with God is only possible after the full rendering of ourselves to him in mystical identification with the suffering and rising with Christ. We see the baskets of loaves from the stories of the feeding of the multitudes, which were early understood (as in John 6) as a foretaste of the heavenly banquet. The banquet here portrayed has several meanings. It refers to the communion of the Liturgy, but also to the funeral agape that followed the Liturgy in the cemeteries, knitting together the living and the dead in one fellowship of the Risen Christ. It refers, too, to the martyr's entrance into heaven and to his participation in the eternal joy of God.

Thus these pictures bring out the fundamental themes of sacrifice—offering, dying, and rising with Christ in the act of "making holy." So, too, in our own Liturgy these are the dominant themes. We offer ourselves by confession, and by the symbolic acts of the collection and of the offering of the bread and wine. It is good that the ancient custom of the congregation offering the bread and wine at the altar is being recovered by the Liturgical Movement. For this brings forcibly to our attention that we there offer our possessions and the work of our hands— not just wheat and grapes, but these made into bread and wine by human industry.

Then in the consecration we relive the dying of the Christ and mystically identify ourselves with the Cross. It is not only a mere "remembering" of it—but a "celebrating" of it before God, a recalling of it so that it is *present* to be effective *in* us. The Cross as an historic act is not, of course, *repeated*. To talk of repeating an act in the past is to talk nonsense. But what we mean is that the eternal reality of the Cross, no less than of the whole work of Christ, is here made present so that it is available to us. Here we become one with the Christ who suffers for the world.

But this "living sacrifice" which we offer in the Divine Victim, who gives himself that we may be given to God in him, finds its consummation in the new life of the heavenly banquet. Here we feast on the life which only comes from death, and become partakers of that Body and Blood which has risen from the dead. Here our self-offering is transformed by God into a new being. We have died to self, to gain a new and different self. We have given our possessions, to receive them again in a new way, no longer enslaved by them. Here we find the true Christian freedom. We are no longer locked in the prison house of our anxiety, getting and spending, planning nervously for an unknown future. Here we are free in God to receive and give as he demands, and to live and die in him. Our security no more is in ourselves; but "made holy" in the sacrificial act, we have passed from death to life, from darkness to light. Now we can face the tragedies that life will offer. Now we can face death itself—for we have found the life in God.

The Christian sacrifice is thus the whole of the Liturgy. In this are comprehended all its themes and movement. Offering, dying, and rising become possible because they are done in Christ, who gives himself in each Eucharist for our salvation. Here ancient sacrifice has been fulfilled and transcended. Here the true act of "making holy" takes place.

EDWARD N. WEST:

The Communion 🕊 7.

Our Lord and his disciples constituted, it is increasingly held today, a special synagogue; and that it was at the *Kiddush,* or the religious meal, of this synagogue that the eucharistic sacrament was instituted; and because of that it was associated with a supper. An example of ancient practice in administering this sacrament was discovered at Constantinople in the nineteenth century. It is a very strange document, known as the *Didache* or *Teaching of the Twelve Apostles.* In all fairness, we do not know the exact date of it, or even its exact setting. It is commonly assumed that it was written either in the late first century or in the early second century. It is certainly a book, or manuscript, devised for the use of a Christian synagogue. Some of it is incredibly beautiful reading, and it comes from the very early Church. It is a temper that we do not know.

Concerning the Eucharist, give thanks in this way. First for the cup; 'We give thanks to thee, our Father, for the holy vine of

David thy servant, which thou madest known to us through thy servant Jesus. To thee be the glory forever.' And for the broken bread; 'We give thanks to thee, our Father, for the life and knowledge, which thou madest known to us through thy servant Jesus. To thee be the glory forever. As this broken bread was scattered upon the hills, and was gathered together and made one, so let thy Church be gathered together into thy kingdom from the ends of the earth; for thine is the glory and the power through Christ Jesus forever!'

Let none eat or drink of your Eucharist, save such as are baptised into the name of the Lord. For concerning this the Lord hath said; 'Give not that which is holy to the dogs.' [1]

It will be noted that in our communion service there are some very hard rubrics or, technically, "cautels" which are printed at the end of the service. In them it is made clear that if a person is "an open and notorious evil liver," the person is to be advertised to the bishop, so that the bishop may excommunicate that person. "Open and notorious evil" living is a highly technical form of sin. This is an illustration of it. In one particular state a most dreadful crime had been committed. It was one of the unspeakable ones. The man who was alleged to have done it (and, by the way, who probably really had done it), was lodged in a tiny jail and in a small town. Popular outrage was such that the local townspeople broke open the jail and lynched the man. The governor of the state, when he heard of it, said that he was "damned glad of it," and the bishop promptly excommunicated him as an "open and notorious evil liver." This is exactly what the words mean. The governor was a warden of one of our parishes. He had taken an oath to maintain the law, and under the law no man is guilty until his peers have declared him so.

The simple problem was this: Should a man, representing the Church—an important man in the organization of the Church—be permitted to say that he was glad of a violation of law, which not only violated every Christian principle behind the law, but also violated the very oath he had taken? The answer is "No." The next question then was, If he cannot, then what does the Church plan to do about it? The Church promptly cut him off from communion with the Body of Christ. (The result was that on the following Sunday, the excommunicated governor stood up in the congregation and made an *open* confession of his sin, and was *openly* reconciled with the Church. This, by the way, is not only a great picture of a bishop, it is also a great picture of a governor. There are few men in public life who respond so quickly and so honorably when a faithless and hideous sin is pointed out.)

To quote further from the *Didache:*

And after ye are filled, give thanks thus: 'We give thee thanks, Holy Father, for thy holy name, which thou hast made to tabernacle in our hearts, and for the knowledge, faith, and immortality which thou hast made known to us through thy servant Jesus. To thee be glory forever. Thou, Lord Almighty, didst create all things for thy name's sake, and gavest food and drink to men for their enjoyment, that they might give thee thanks; and to us thou didst grant spiritual food and drink and life eternal through thy servant. Above all we thank thee that thou art mighty. To thee be glory forever. Remember, Lord, thy Church, to deliver her from all evil and to make her perfect in thy love, and to gather from the four winds her that is sanctified into thy kingdom which thou didst prepare for her; for thine is the power and the glory forever. Let grace come, and let this world pass away. Hosanna to the God of David. If any is holy, let him come: if any is not holy, let him repent. *Maranatha.* Amen.'

And then this:

On the Lord's day assemble and break bread and give thanks, having first confessed your sins that your sacrifice may be pure. If any have a dispute with his fellow, let him not come to the assembly till they be reconciled, that your sacrifice be not polluted. For this is the sacrifice spoken of by the Lord; 'In every place and at every time offer to me a pure sacrifice; for I am a great king, said the Lord, and my name is wonderful among the Gentiles . . .'

Elect therefore for yourselves bishops and deacons worthy of the Lord, men that are gentle and not covetous, true men and approved; for they also minister to you the ministry of the prophets and teachers. Therefore, despise them not; for these are they that are honored of you with the prophets and teachers . . .

This marked insistence on having the bishops and deacons as spiritual officers tends to date this particular book.

Hysteria has always been near to religion and to religious expression. In primitive religions indeed, hysteria not only existed and was recognized, but was quite frankly, induced. There are recorded in the New Testament occurrences of what, nowadays, we would just term hysterical religion. This, by the way, does not mean that they are not religious—let us be honest about that—but it does mean that they are overtones of minds which have moved slightly out of connection with the world in which we live. St. Paul had to face this. Prophets were highly regarded, but these prophets were not *prophets* in our sense of the word. They neither foretold nor told forth the will of God, but rather were given to "tongues." "Tongues" were strange, hysterical sounds which in human terms made no sense. St. Paul, in the great thirteenth chapter of I Corinthians, goes out of his way to make it clear that no matter how fully one has these charismatic gifts, or even how much one has of ordinary faith—to the point of being able to move mountains—if one lacks charity, then the gifts do not really matter. From St. Paul's point of view, the word *charity* is synonymous with the word *Christ*. One ought to read that thirteenth chapter of I Corinthians, substituting the word *Christ* for *charity* all the way through (changing *itself* to *himself* and *her* to *his*, to understand St. Paul's exact meaning).

The early Church had not had good experience with "prophets," which has dictated their loss to the Christian ministry. In the ordinary sense we do not have a charismatic ministry now; we have only the regular commissioned officers of that "regular army" which is the Body of Christ. Today, in general, we tend to find them, more than anywhere else, in some of the smaller or non-liturgical groups in this country. Where they do exist, they still make the same sounds, and go through the same kinds of physical motions which were characteristic of the early Church. One of the most distinguished Quakers in the country said that the real problem with Quakerism was this: A man starts out by saying that he has a personal relationship with God which, we hope, *is* true. He then moves on from that to the statement that he has a special relationship with God, which *may*, or may not, be true. He ends up by saying that he has a private line with God, and that is *not* true! This story is characteristic of the danger of charismatic ministry. It means that all the mixed motives in the human mind can become terribly involved, and that a man moved by hysteria too often hears the echo of his own voice and mistakes it for the voice of God. The Church did not prosper under this, and it wanted its regular administrative officers, the ones originally instituted to get the work done, to become its spiritual officers. There were bishops in the first days of the Church, but these bishops were "over-seers" of the Church's work. They were the ones who got the work done. The deacons, who were the immediate servants of the bishops, were the ones who went out and ministered to the poor, who took to the Church's poor their portions of the offerings. They administered the Church's charity. The episcopate—the bishops—were much the same as the rulers of synagogues had been. The deacon, in general, was much the same as the *minister* in the synagogue. The *presbyteroi*, the presbyters, were still a council of elders—a college which had general charge of the congregation.

If one wishes to talk about bishops in terms which make sense to Episcopalians, it must be remembered that the bishop's first job in the world was to be president of the Eucharist. To talk about Apostolic Succession, and to talk with any mature intelligence in the matter, it must be noted that being an apostle meant being able to witness to the Risen Lord; and a bishop, as the president of the Eucharist, actually presides over the very function through which we know the Risen Lord in the breaking of bread. The Eucharist is the continuing Resurrection appearance. When a bishop is consecrated, he is commissioned by the historic body of Christ in this world, but he is also examined to make certain, as far as man can know, that he has been called of the Lord Jesus to do this work right now. He is, first and foremost, to be a living witness to the Resurrection of his Lord. If one wished to argue Apostolic Succession on those terms, one is on absolutely safe ground. If one wishes to argue apostolic succession in terms of Church government, the argument is already lost. There have been periods in Church history—particularly, for example, in the ancient Church of Ireland—in which the administration of a Diocese was in the hands of an abbot or a vicar-general, and the bishop was exactly what he had been originally, a spiritual officer.

Any bishop, in our day, will say that the hardest thing which goes with his task is the separation which his job imposes, separation between himself and his people. He has to get the work of the Church done; he was elected and consecrated to get the work done. He has to have an opinion on public affairs; he must be an informed man; he must have a mind capable of dealing with great public problems involving faith and morals. Often a bishop's only parish is his clergy; and since both he and his clergy are hardworking men, far too often his only moment of intimacy and friendship even with them, comes when there is trouble. When there is illness, or death, or some other terrible thing, he is again able to minister to people—otherwise, not. This is too great a burden to put upon a man whose first and foremost reason for being is that he is a living witness to the resurrection of his Lord and ours.

The *Didache* was written to make people understand that, much as they valued prophets, they should be ready to accept the spiritual ministry of bishops and deacons. Spiritual ministry existed to offer sacrifice, and Christianity had a real sacrifice to offer. We have a real sacrifice with a real communion involved. The communion is not only with God, however; nor is it only with bread and wine; it is also one with one another. Hence the stern moral requirements, which became law under Justinian, are still in our Prayer Book. If people cannot get along with each other, then something must be done about it, because they are destroying the communion! They are eating and drinking the Body and Blood of Christ to their own damnation, "not discerning the Lord's Body". To think that one can find God's Body in heaven, which one has not seen, or find God's Body in bread and wine, and yet deny God's Body wherever else that Body appears—in the sacred Body of Christ—is totally to deceive oneself.

Our service involves something which is to serve us *until* our Lord comes again. The ultimate thing is totally different. One can read of it in the Revelation of St. John the Divine—which is a sort of word-picture of the theology of the Epistle to the Hebrews. The theology of Hebrews concentrates on our Lord as the high priest. This has behind it the Gospel of St. John. St. Paul's thinking, of course, is concentrated on Christ as the victim, the Lamb slain before the foundation of the world—something which was done once and for all. It is "the once and for all" idea which stands behind all real sacrifice. To the Jew, the making of a real sacrifice did not mean God's doing the same act again each year. Real sacrifice meant making memorial of the Passover. Real sacrifice, for the Christian, does not mean killing Christ all over again, and making our God a creature bound by our time and space—we cannot do that. Christ is the Lamb slain before the foundation of the world, and this Lamb revealed himself by being slain once and for all in our world. We make sacrifice by offering the memorial of that—the memorial which he has commanded. The communion service is not devised to pull God down into our atmosphere—it is rather, as Bishop Frere said, "an excursion of the congregation into eternity." All of a sudden, for a moment, we are living our real life. All of a sudden, for a moment, we see others as they really are. All of a sudden, for a moment, that most unbelievable of things, we see ourselves as we really are.

Our communion service is a combination of ordinary synagogue worship and the liturgy of the Upper Room. The early Church did not have the penitential quality which we have. The early Church was, as Dr. Richardson has reminded us, simply filled with joy. When the clergy came in, there was a hymn known as the *Kyrie*, that which we translate as "Lord have mercy upon us, Christ have mercy upon us, Lord have mercy upon us." The first section refers to the Father; the second obviously refers to Christ; and (the third time the word *Lord* is used) refers to the Holy Ghost. This ancient practice is witnessed to in Pliny's strange statement that the Christians met before daybreak "to recite a hymn antiphonally, to Christ, as to a God." Unfortunately, in the Western Church, it is impossible to translate *Kyrie eleison* and convey the impression which the early Church would receive from that phrase. An ordinary Greek community, when the emperor came into town, would turn out and roar at the top of their lungs, "*Kyrie eleison. Kyrie eleison.*" This was an exclamation upon the *nature* of the emperor. This was, therefore, for the early Church, an observation on the Lord whose nature it was to be merciful. As Westerners, we have gradually made this acclamation penitential. In terms of music, the most perfect expression of the Western Church's thinking in this matter is the Kyrie from the *Missa Marialis*. It is the haunting cry of an absolutely abject soul. It is one of the most beautiful things in the world, and it is exactly what the early Church did *not* mean. The Eastern mind is best conveyed by a great Russian choir singing the fortyfold *Gospode pomilui,* which is the Russian translation of *Kyrie eleison*. It is a musical essay into the nature of God; it runs all the way up and down the scale; its dynamics are unbelievable. It starts with great shouts then dies away to nothing, and comes back to end with great shouts of joy. It is a symphony on the mercy of God. Another form of *Kyrie,* which was used as an Introit on the very great days by the Mozarabic Rite, and certain other Western rites, was the extended one we know as the *Gloria in excelsis*—it is an expanded *Kyrie*. The references to the Father, to Christ, and to the Holy Spirit are all filled in.

It is only fair to say that when Christian liturgics is confronted with any two possible alternatives, it chooses all three. Therefore, since these forms of the *Kyrie* were alternative in the early Western Church, we end up by having them sequential. In the medieval mass, the *Kyrie,* on any festival day, was followed immediately by the *Gloria in excelsis*. (The position of the *Gloria,* and consequently the position of the ablutions, in the 1552 Prayer Book are, as we know, due to Cranmer's thinking. It was a move which was not ill-considered.)

After this Introit in the early Church, they went on to review the mighty acts of God. There was, therefore, an Old Testament lection. It is one of the riches we have lost; and a real loss it is. Unless we have at least the truncated

form of Morning Prayer immediately before the communion service, we have no account of the actions of our God
with our ancient fathers—Abraham, Isaac, and Israel were
our fathers too. *We* are the people of God; *we* are the people delivered at the Red Sea. *We* are the people to whom
the Lord was given. Anything less than this view is simply
not Christian!

After this review of the mighty acts of God, there followed the ancient songs from Israel's hymnal, the Psalter.
Special litanies were then said on behalf of all of God's people. We now have their concluding prayer, known as the
Collect. A collect gets its name because it collects or sums
up the prayers which had just been said in the litany. (It
has nothing to do with the Epistle or the Gospel.) That
being done, more songs were sung, and then came a reading from one of the Epistles. This was addressed to the
faithful, since it was good advice, and, often, admonitions
as to how to be faithful in Christ's religion.

After this came more songs, and then the *first* of the
manifestations of the Word of God. The Gospeller received the Book of the Gospels at the altar, and then went
to a special place in order to read from it. (In our service
we continue the ancient practice of addressing the Book
itself with the phrase, "Glory be to thee, O Lord.") The
Book itself is sacred; it is the Word of God. In the ancient
Church, and still in the Eastern Church, a bishop at this
point takes off his pallium—since he has no right to wear
a vestment symbolic of authority when God himself is
speaking. This is a fine piece of Christian liturgics.

The Word of God was, after this, normally ministered
in its *second* way, preaching. Preaching ranks very highly

in the New Testament. It is assumed, however, that this is preaching connected with the Body of Christ and the Good News which has just been proclaimed. In the early Church it would have been unthinkable that any man would preach on anything other than the Scripture. This is what he was there for; this was an essential part of his ministry.

After the preaching, the Church moved on to the sacred Mystery—the Liturgy of the Upper Room—which comprised the offertory and the consecration of the gifts.

Before all of this, in our American Prayer Book, we, as part of the great Western Church, have a penitential beginning. Our communion service begins with the Collect for Purity, and either the Decalogue or the Summary of the Law. The *Kyrie,* as we use it, must be viewed very largely as a solemn, rather than a festive, form of preparation. There are historic reasons. The early Church, as we noted in the *Didache,* expected the Lord to come in his second Advent immediately. They lived constantly in the expectation that it might be "today," and they looked forward to this with passionate joy. Gradually it became clear that the hand of God was going to manifest itself differently from the way they expected. The author of Revelation never for a moment thought that God would end the dreadful persecution of Christians in any manner other than by coming down with lightnings and thunder to blast the wretched persecutors off the face of the earth. It never crossed his mind that God might ultimately have an emperor baptized in the Name of the Lord Jesus. Yet this is the way it worked out. When the Church moved into the Western world, it was dealing with barbarians—

our ancestors. Most of them were Christianized in a highly effective missionary way, but the beneficial results were not always immediately apparent. A great prince leading an army was defeated, and the army was given the choice of being baptized or beheaded. One could count on a fair number of converts. These people were now, according to all the rules, part of the Body of Christ. The day before they were pagans, murderers, and adulterers; now they were part of the Body of Christ, but still murderers and adulterers. It posed a real problem since the Church could take nothing for granted. These rough converts had to be reminded over and over again of the moral implications of Christianity. Thus the whole penitential note came into our Western thinking. (Moral honesty is one of the gifts of our people, and the suggestion that we omit from the communion service the Invitation, Confession, Absolution, and Comfortable Words, makes them quite unhappy. One of the things which bothers our people is the haunting problem of worthiness. So many of our people don't feel worthy of making their communion. Actually none of us is! If the performance of a service depended on worthiness, what man would dare to stand at any altar? Fortunately, it doesn't. It depends solely on the nature of our God— a nature which is endlessly forgiving and endlessly loving.)

In the Offertory following the practice of the ancient Church, we not only offer our gifts and our money, but also an accounting of the way in which we use the rest of the money that we do not give, not only our time, but also an accounting of how we use the time we do not spend in church. We are appearing before One who is not deceived; we offer *exactly* what we are! It constitutes a fairly shoddy loaf of bread. If each of us were represented by some kind of grain in that loaf, there might be a high vitamin content, but it would be pretty dark in color. What is being offered is us, just as we are. Yet Christ our God offers this to the Father, and the Father's nature is such that he finds this offering perfectly acceptable. We offer ourselves; and then we are offered by our Lord, in such complete union with him that his life, his acts, and his spirit become our life, our acts, our spirit. This is what worship really means.

After we have offered these, we have in the American Prayer Book, the Prayer for the Church. It is a prayer for its *whole state*—which means its healthy condition. This has become for us a prayer of intention: a statement of the objects for which these gifts are being offered. This is very important, since we must be certain that our prayer is "common" enough to include *all* the persons who make up the Body of Christ.

We must always remember that God is not in the slightest degree dependent on our words! There is no more virtue in word-magic than there is in any other kind of magic. Magic is the enemy of religion. We do what we do, because God Incarnate ordered us to do it. We express what we express, because in our immediate family in the Body of Christ this is the way we have known our Lord.

The Invitation which follows does not invite even Episcopalians to make their communion. The invitation is entirely concerned with charity and morality. It demands the leading of a new life, the strict following of the commandments of God from that very moment. It demands that we walk in his holy ways, repent of our sins, and be in love and charity with our neighbor. If we can respond to these challenges, we need to say something about them. If we can't, the alternative is not that it is too bad; the alternative is damnation! We are not "discerning" the Lord's Body.

Our form of Confession is not for our own particular sins; rather it is for the sins which we as the membership of the Body of Christ have committed—bad housing, injustice all around us, not only in other states, but in our own city and in our own neighborhoods and, often, God forgive us, in our own parishes, and even in our own families. It is our constant failure to recognize in other members of our own family the image of our God.

Following this Confession, we receive the assurance of our Lord's merciful nature, and the forgiveness of the Church. This, however, requires more than just a statement. If one is to appropriate the forgiveness offered, it means that one has to have the courage to do so. It has been pointed out that it is not only more blessed to give than it is to receive, but it is much easier! We are all trained in giving, and we do it so graciously that we often admire ourselves in the course of the process. It is such a happy posture. Yet how badly we receive. The same is true of forgiveness. It is easy enough to arrive at the point where we can forgive somebody else. We may even arrive at the point where we believe God *can* forgive us. That, however, is not good enough. We must arrive at the point where we can forgive ourselves. This takes real courage, because it means looking at ourselves exactly as we are. It means seeing for a moment, in this wretched little thing, something which is of infinite concern to the God of the universe. The *Words* need to be "comfortable"—encouraging.

The *Sursum corda,* "Lift up your hearts," is not a step in pulling God down. It is the exact reverse. Our whole service is an essay in Resurrection and Ascension. We had started down where we really were, but now we are being caught up into the life of the Trinity. ("Let us give thanks unto our Lord God" and its response come from the Hebrew blessing of the Cup.) The Preface reminds us as to why we are praising our God, and then follows the *Sanctus,* the "Holy, Holy, Holy," which comes from the Third Benediction of Israel.

The most important item in our liturgy is, of course, the Prayer of Consecration. The wording in the American Prayer Book is that of the 1549 Prayer Book—Cranmer's wording, very largely—but done in the order of the Liturgy of St. James. This is an inheritance we have from the Scottish Non-Juring Bishops. Our first American bishop, Samuel Seabury, was consecrated by Scottish bishops, and they insisted, as the only price of their consecrating him, that the American Church would take on the ancient full Liturgy of St. James, which they themselves used. This is different from the English Prayer Book. The English Prayer Book of 1662 is, like the 1549 one, basically both Western and medieval in its approach. In that Book the Words of Institution constitute the actual consecration. This is not true of the Liturgy of St. James. Our Prayer Book works on a far more complicated, and far more ancient, theory of liturgics. We must never attempt, however, to un-church half of Christendom because they do not use the same liturgy as we. That would be to forget who is actually doing the consecrating—God, the Holy Spirit, is quite capable of bypassing any combination of words, even ours.

The Liturgy, which we have, has the reminder that the sacrament was set up to last us only until he comes again. We then have the account of what he did at supper on the night in which he was betrayed. This is the "intention" for what is to happen on Good Friday, in which the great sacrifice was to be given once and for all—"a full, perfect, and sufficient sacrifice, oblation, and satisfaction, for the sins of the whole world."

The Oblation *is* the sacrifice. This is the making memorial of our Lord's incarnation, of his sacrifice, of his acts. We offer the holy gifts as he commanded us to do, but we do it in remembrance of his passion and death, his mighty resurrection, and his glorious ascension. We then move on to the Invocation, in which we pray that the gifts may be caught up into the life of the Trinity. Our phrase in English is just a little awkward. It reads this way: "And we most humbly beseech thee, O merciful Father, to hear us; and, of thy almighty goodness, vouchsafe to bless and sanctify, with thy Word and Holy Spirit, these thy gifts and creatures of bread and wine . . ." The following is not as good English, but it is far clearer: "And we most humbly beseech thee, O merciful Father, to hear us; and of thy almighty goodness, together with thy Word and Holy Spirit, to bless and sanctify these thy gifts and creatures of bread and wine." It is an action of the whole Trinity. This is what is required as necessary as a declaration of what we think we are doing, and what our God is doing in and through his Church.

There is still something more however: we must, in

the words of the early Church, "be made *one*" with our Christ. That is why the phrase, deriving ultimately from the Liturgy of St. Basil, is so important. It is the one in which prayer is offered that the recipients of the sacrament, "may worthily receive the most precious Body and Blood of thy Son Jesus Christ, be filled with thy grace and heavenly benediction, and made one body with him, that he may dwell in us, and we in him." This is a prayer that we may be united to the most precious Body and Blood of our Christ.

We conclude the Consecration by saying the prayer which Christ himself taught us to pray. In response to the breaking of bread, we acknowledge the Resurrection of our Lord in the prayer which follows. The layman has the right instinct in his devotion to the Prayer of Humble Access. The instinct is right, because this prayer recognizes the reunion of the Body and the Blood. The reunion of body and blood *is* resurrection! That is why we kneel and say this incredibly magnificent prayer. What we are saying is that we who have known the Risen Lord in the breaking of bread, now find him in its broken fragments. Any religion short of that is not really mature.

In making our Communion, it is not only communion with our Lord in some rarefied spiritual sense, but in a most physical sense. This is real bread and real wine, which, by the mystery of our God, have been made the media for conveying the life-giving sacrament of his own Body and Blood. We also have communion one with another. To fail in any one of these three is to hold a faulty theology; it is failure to discern the Lord's Body.

Cranmer's theory in putting the *Gloria in excelsis* at

the end of the service was to restore the pure apostolic note of joy—unbounded joy. It was for that reason that the elements were not consumed; they were left on the altar for purposes of thanksgiving. This is evident, even more markedly, in the English Prayer Book. The sacrament is consecrated quickly by the use of the Words of Institution, and when all have communicated, the Lord's Prayer is said by people who are sacramentally entitled to call God, Father. That is the power of the English Prayer Book. The power of our own is, of course, the incredible beauty of its spelling out of the full spiritual implication of the Eucharist.

Were someone to ask, "What is the Episcopal Church's theory about consecration?" it would be perfectly fair to say that this church has *no* theory about consecration. Were someone to say, "May I believe in transubstantiation?" the answer would be, "Yes—you just cannot require me to do it." Were one to ask, "May I believe in consubstantiation?" the answer would be, "Well, if you can believe that, in spite of what the words say, I don't mind." The point is our church's characteristic hatred of precise definition. We always feel that precise definition clouds truth. The French statement, *Un dieu defini, c'est un dieu fini,* is perfectly sound. "Do we believe in real presence?" We certainly do! "Do we have a theory as to how it gets that way?" We certainly do not! What we say is that God, because of his act, starts with our gifts and us, as we are, and by the mystery of his sacrament, ends up by giving us back our gifts and ourselves as they and we ought to be. The change effected is, what Archbishop Temple would call, "trans-evaluation." Our gifts start out as bread; they end up by being more than bread. We start out as not quite human; we end up a lot more than human. Indeed, we almost, at this split second of pure worship, become normal. It is not as though we were normal, and Christ was supernormal; we, natural, and Christ, supernatural. It is rather that Christ is normal, and most of us most of the time are subnormal. We only become normal when we are at one with him!

III. ৯৶

In His Hand

LESLIE J. A. LANG:

The Assuring Hand:
Absolution ॐ   *8.*

There was brought to Jesus one day a man sick of the palsy, lying on a bed. Our Lord looked on that man and saw beneath the physical infirmity, perhaps mysteriously entangled with it, a spiritual disease so great that shaking limbs were but the outward manifestation of a soul trembling and powerless to act or move with that freedom which is the service of God. Those who brought this man to Jesus evidently perceived in our Lord one who had power over the forces of sin, suffering, and sickness, for he said to the sick of the palsy, "Son, be of good cheer; thy sins be forgiven thee." And to certain scribes in the company, who quite as evidently saw in Jesus a blasphemer, he said, "But that ye may know that the Son of man hath power on earth to forgive sins [and here he addressed himself to the sick of the palsy], 'Arise, take up thy bed, and go unto thine house.' And he arose, and departed to his house." (Matt. 9:1-8)

That the Son of man has power on this earth to forgive sins is the necessary conviction of every Christian, for it is the declared message of the Gospel. The words of the dying Saviour, "Father, forgive them," have always been the undying assurance that in Jesus' death there is forgiveness and grace to amend our sinful lives. That this power and grace have been mediated through the Mystical Body of which Jesus Christ is the Head, as it was mediated through his physical body in this scene at Capernaum, has been the conviction of the Church whenever it has lived up to her Prayer Book name of Catholic, "holding earnestly the Faith for all times, in all countries, and for all people," as she has preached the whole Gospel to the whole world. (BCP, p. 291)

The manner in which the proclamation of this truth has been made, the words spoken, the methods used, the outward signs and accompaniments employed, the explanation of how it is so, the disciplines and the sacramental signs, all have varied with the times. Their long succession began in the earliest days of the Christian community with a question which stirred, with bewilderment and fear, the hearts and minds of those who had "put on" Christ; for one of the earliest "religious issues" was the uncertainty as to whether, after turning from darkness unto light, after being buried with Christ in Baptism to rise to newness of life, any sin could ever again be forgiven. So pressing was the question and so real the fear that, although infant baptism was taught, adult baptism long remained the norm; and for countless Christians the day of death became the day of baptism. Mercifully, the question was answered and the fear mitigated when a penitential system was set up for those who had responded to Christ and, as is common to the best of us, failed him. In spite of those who held that such failure was apostasy, and therefore unforgivable, public confession was provided, and public penance required at least for what were regarded as the sins of gravity or scandal.

One could trace the process historically and one would see that as the Church came out from underground, and Christianity became a permitted and legal religion, and numbers increased, public confession and penance became as offensive as the sins committed. By the time of the Middle Ages, private confession before God in the presence of a priest (heard by, spoken into the ear of the priest, hence the term "auricular confession") became not only the norm but the required discipline. It is claimed by some historians that this practice is the contribution of the British monasteries to the rest of the Christian world. The distinction between the graver and lesser sins remained ("mortal" sins and "venial" sins they were called), but in practice it soon became a distinction without a difference, as those who hear confessions could testify.

There are many among us who would hold the opinion that all of this came to an end at the Reformation, and that except for some odd people at odd times in odd places, we all go to confession, but quite out in the open, every Sunday, using the words provided for that purpose in the Book of Common Prayer. The truth of the matter is that the practice of private confession and absolution privately pronounced never ceased in the Anglican Communion. We have written evidence of penitents and confessors from the sixteenth century until now. We have the recorded words of Anglican teachers and divines of all the past four centuries.

The Church of England has canon laws with respect to this practice, notably one which bids the priests' lips to keep silence. By general concurrence the Sacrament of Absolution is being made increasingly available to our people, by whatever name it passes: confession, penance, "spiritual counsel," or "a priest will be in church every Saturday from four to five."

This may be the situation, but the situation must be judged by the truth. For us Episcopalians all the truth necessary to salvation is to be found in Holy Scriptures. The question, therefore, may rightly be asked: Does the New Testament teach us that in the divine dispensation there is a provision for what we know as the sacrament of Absolution? Is "confession" to be found in the Gospel? If by that is meant, do we find there the direct command from our Lord, "Go to confession!" or a formula for carrying it out, then the inevitable answer is "No." (But if that were the end of the matter, there would be no need for this discussion of Absolution.)

The uneasiness about Absolution is based upon the suspicion that somehow this sacramental practice places a man between our souls and God, thus denying us free and unencumbered access to his grace. But there *is* a *man* between our souls and God, the Man, Christ Jesus. He, "who for us men and for our salvation came down from heaven . . . was made man," the great Sacrament of God. When the Church acts in his name it is acting as God acts, for it is acting in the name of Jesus, through outward and visible signs of an inward and spiritual grace. Now God is the giver of sacraments and not their servant. He can and does save by the "baptism of desire" as well as baptism with water.

He makes himself present even to those who never go to Holy Communion, but both of these sacraments are of divine institution, and both are administered by man in Christ's name. In the sacrament of Absolution the Lamb of God who takes away the sins of the world, and who is ever ready to forgive the sins of the contrite, makes present at a specific time and place, for a specific person, the assurance of his forgiveness which is ever freely offered; just as in Holy Communion, he who is ever and everywhere present makes himself known especially for those who are gathered together in a particular time, at a particular place, in the breaking of bread. God, in Absolution, speaks the word of forgiveness. For God to speak is for God to act, and in speaking the word he extends the assuring Hand of release from the burden of guilt. It is right, therefore, that provision is made for this ministry in the Prayer Book.

When the bishop is admonished at his consecration to "heal the sick," certainly there is implied the ministry of reconciliation of sick souls to God.

The words spoken by the bishop as he lays hands upon the priest-to-be in ordination obviously apply directly to the subject of our consideration:

Receive the Holy Ghost for the Office and Work of a Priest in the Church of God, now committed unto thee by the Imposition of our hands. Whose sins thou dost forgive, they are forgiven: whose sins thou dost retain, they are retained. And be thou a faithful Dispenser of the Word of God, and of his holy Sacraments; In the Name of the Father, and of the Son, and of the Holy Ghost. Amen. (BCP, p. 546)

These gospel words, "retaining" and "forgiving", concern, in this connection, the whole matter of godly discipline within the Church; but they have been traditionally interpreted as including the ministry of Absolution, and for that reason they are in this place in the Prayer Book. One notes, also, how they are immediately followed by a reference to God's Word and the Sacraments.

In the Order for the Visitation of the Sick, the Priest may, "as occasion demands," move the sick person "to make a special confession of his sins." (BCP, p. 313) Surely, one would not say that the Prayer Book thereby limits this ministry to a deathbed repentance, or even to the "seriousness" of the sickness, which is not always easy to measure.

That the Prayer Book does not do so is evidenced by the further provision for confession and absolution in the second Exhortation following the Order for Holy Communion:

And because it is requisite that no man should come to the holy Communion, but with a full trust in God's mercy, and with a quiet conscience; therefore, if there be any of you, *who by this means cannot quiet* his own conscience herein, but requireth further comfort or counsel, let him come to me, or to some other Minister of God's Word, and open his grief; that he may receive such godly counsel and advice, as may tend to the quieting of his conscience, and the removing of all scruple and doubtfulness. (BCP, p. 87-8)

In the First Prayer Book the Exhortation, at this point, included the word "absolution";[1] and one may wonder whether, in a young nation which had so recently achieved its independence, and was struggling with the notion that all men are equal before God, our fathers were not a bit shy about any misunderstanding concerning any kind of power of one over another, including "priestly power."

Opinions as to the necessity and frequency and universality of the application of this Prayer Book provision and privilege may differ, and in this as in all matters, our liberty is that with which Christ has made us free; but on the basis of Anglican formularies and practice of more than four hundred years one draws two conclusions: first, that the ministry of Absolution is one of the normal elements in the Church's ministry to souls, that it is in accordance with Anglican teaching, that it is rooted in the Gospel, that it is one of the ways in which God holds out his *assuring hand,* and that by a true instinct it is presented to us as a sacramental means of grace; second, in contradistinction to the sacraments of Baptism and Holy Communion it is not "generally necessary to salvation," i.e., necessary for everybody; but like Holy Matrimony and Holy Orders, it is to be used for a special purpose and vocation. For some it is a means of carrying out that general vocation to holiness, a means without which they, at least, cannot see the Lord.

The classic Anglican position has been stated often since the seventeenth century in the familiar words: "None must, all may, some should." The burden of such compulsion as there may be always rests upon the individual. He may say, "I must," but never, "You must." The compulsion is always moral, never legal. The discipline must be self-imposed, for there will always be those whose consciences cry out, "How shall we escape, if we neglect so great salvation . . . ?" (Hebrews 2:3) With due allowance for liberty of conscience it is the considered opinion of an ever increasing number of those responsible for the teaching office of the Church, and of those "who are grieved and wearied with the burden of . . . sins," that the children of God, be they young or old, should at least know what is meant by the "benefit of absolution." Many a pastor can testify that the word about this spoken in the long past has been remembered afterwards—unto salvation.

And in a day when God is granting us a special vision of "how good and joyful a thing it is for brethren to dwell together in unity," it is incumbent upon every one of us to value those "treasures," to some of us "old," and to others "new," which we have in common with one another, within the Episcopal Church, and with "our separated brethren."

There is no particular kind of religion peculiar to the Episcopal Church, and the former Archbishop of Canterbury, Dr. Geoffrey Fisher, has stated that we hold the only Faith there is, the Catholic Faith of the historic Creeds. And so we go to traditional statements of moral theology, and to such manuals for confessors and penitents as are available, to seek such technical words and standard definitions as this occasion requires that we should call to mind. The *subject* of the sacrament of Absolution is a baptized person who, with reasonable knowledge of what he is doing and true repentance, confesses his sins. (It should be noted that in the General Confession in the Liturgy we confess *sin;* in the sacrament of Absolution we confess *sins*.) The *matter* of the sacrament is what we truly remember and honestly admit. The *form*, or "outward sign," of the sacrament is a formula of absolution, a common one being, "I absolve thee from all thy sins." The *effect* of the sacrament is the assurance of God's grace and forgiveness. The *"seal* of confession," as it is called, is the requirement that what is spoken shall not be revealed to others.

The minister of the sacrament is one in Priest's Orders, and it is always to be remembered that he is but the minister, one among us who serves in the name of Christ, and on behalf of "the blessed company of all faithful people." Since we are members one of another, an offense against God, or even against oneself, is an offense against all. But only God can ultimately forgive, in the sense that it is ultimately against God that we sin. And let us be sure that we know what forgiveness means. It is the assurance that we are released and discharged from guilt, that we are acquitted, justified, that something comes to an end that a new life may begin, and it is God alone who does this.

That "confession is good for the soul" few people today would doubt, for it has a certain backing in the fields of psychology and psychiatry and psychoanalysis; but it is none of these, and more than these, though it may serve some of their ends, and in some cases (but not all) make the resort to them unnecessary. In the sacrament of Absolution the prodigal son returns to his father. He "comes to himself." He says, "I will arise and go to my father." He tells him, "I am no more worthy to be called thy son; make me as one of thy hired servants." That is, he is contrite; he confesses; he makes amends. But when his mind is first made up, "when he is yet a great way off," his father sees him, and goes out to meet him with the outstretched and assuring hand. He is forgiven; he is set free. He is restored to his father's company and to his family. This is Absolution.[2]

For those of a childlike heart it is as simple as that; but for those of us who are caught up in the stress and strain of these days, whose lives either because of sin, or circumstances, or sophistication, or the erosion of time are far from childlike, the process is the same, and the end is the same. The sacrament of Absolution can better enable us to live with one another, and with God, but also with ourselves. For most of us have to live with our own limitations, and those limitations, in great measure, will follow us to the end. We know that "we can do all things through Christ who strengthens us," but it is no weakness of faith to face the fact that this must mean all things that are possible to us. As year succeeds to year and what lies ahead is beyond our comprehension, when moral alternatives become increasingly more difficult to meet or even to discern, when in society and sometimes within us, sin, sickness, and suffering are joined together as once they were on that day in Capernaum, and we may think that we are almost powerless against the evils that do beset us, then the ministry of Absolution bears witness that if I will come to him, God will take me by the hand, and will assure me that if I cannot always do the best, then by his grace, I can do the best that is possible for me.

To defend a truth, or even to explain it, is in itself not enough. There remains one thing more which must be said.

If, by chance, in the sacrament of Absolution, I hear the
Gospel Word spoken, if there I hear "good news" for me,
then let me go away with the psalmist's assurance in my
inmost heart:

> Though I walk in the midst of trouble,
> yet shalt thou refresh me;
> thou shalt stretch forth thy hand
> upon the furiousness of mine enemies,
> and thy right hand shall save me. (Psalm 138:7)

JOHN ELLIS LARGE:

The Healing Hand:
Unction ૯➤   9.

Spiritual healing is God's restoration of wholeness to a
human personality—a wholeness of which soul, mind, and
body are integral parts; it is the renewal of the inner man.
It constituted an astonishingly large part of Christ's public
ministry. Indeed, to read the Gospels just as they come,
healing seemed to be the chief thing for which Jesus was
known by the ordinary people of his day. To vary slightly
a phrase of Alan Richardson's: Spiritual healing is Love in
power reaching out to love in need. Faith and repentance
generally marked the recipients of Christ's healing, but there
are other instances in which the only characteristic was
a dread sense of need—"Lord, help me!" To quote *Prayer
Book Studies* III, The Order for the Ministration to the
Sick: "There is no evidence that Christ thought of any
sickness as incurable, or limited his ministrations to what
we call functional disorders. He healed the blind, the

leper, the paralyzed, the crippled, and the mentally diseased." [1] All this, for the man of our own day, raises the
problem of the credibility of the New Testament account.
Did Jesus really heal? Do such healings happen today?
What about the physician? How much of this healing
is "psychological"? If it works, how does it work?

There is no competent New Testament scholar in the
world who makes any case against the authenticity of the
several texts which describe Jesus' healings. The question
is not whether the texts are original, but rather whether
they describe something which is true. To this question,
there is but one honest answer: if it can be done now, then
I'm obligated to face the possibility that he could do it
then.

Are we really convinced, however, that, even assuming
a man gets better, his real illness had any spiritual root?

It's a commonplace these days to remind ourselves
that man is made up of a trinity. But we act as though we
really meant that man is merely a duality of body and mind.
We may tip our hat as a courtesy to the spirit, but we
spend the vast majority of our time with the mind and
the body. And therein lies our common tragedy.[2]

We think of ourselves as smart in the ways of the
scientific management of our brains and of our flesh, and
smart we indeed may be. But it is our crowning stupidity
that we brush off the one element of the trinity which
alone gives fullest meaning and fulfillment to the other
two. This matter of the spirit is admittedly a much more
subtle business than the all too obvious body is. But it's
always the subtleties in life which point the obvious factors
to their rightful destiny.

A neglected or disaffected spirit can poison the body no less fatally than can a lethal dose of a corroding acid. And until we face the fact that man's spirit needs at least as much nourishment and attention as his body and brain do, we shall go on needlessly, like egregious fools, crippling and killing ourselves.

There is plainly nothing tangible about the spirit of God as it broods within, and hovers over, the human frame. Yet it is the tangible which is always transitory, and the intangible which is the abiding.

Dr. Russell G. MacRobert, an eminent New York physician specializing in psychiatry and neurology, has put the matter this way:

There is an area that is beyond the ken of the scientist—an extra-scientific realm. It can be called the spiritual world, the psychic universe or what not; but call it what you will, it is an area of the universe in which at present we can look for guidance only to poets, lovers, psychics, and seers. But it is real, possibly more real than the world about us which we can see and touch.

Mystery surrounds the more profound things of life, such as birth, death, love and resurrection. When we demand categorical and scientific proof of God, our souls start to shrivel, and the Lord of whom we demand the mathematician's Q.E.D. thereupon either becomes useless to us or we to him. When a man loses the sense of awesome wonder in the face of life, he loses life itself.

So it is with the Church's sacramental ministry of healing. No modern man—however deep his dedication or lengthy his experience in the field—can call himself an expert in this sphere of pastoral care. The most that the best of us can do is to try humbly to recapture the lost radiance of what was once a relatively common phenomenon as recorded in the pages of the New Testament, and by the generations immediately thereafter.

Ours is truly a sacramental world. A completely disembodied spirit is unknown and unknowable. We have immortal souls, but they are clothed in mortal bodies. It is by means of the physical that we apprehend the spiritual. When a man raises his hat to a lady, that is a sacramental gesture in acknowledgment of her womanhood, as well as of her actual or potential motherhood. A handshake is sacramental, since it is an outward token of a reality felt in the heart. A kiss, the very act of love, is sacramental in character. By Christ's own promise and command, water becomes the channel of his blessing upon the recipient. So, also, bread and wine are used in Holy Communion by our Lord's own direction. Yet these common elements are destined to become the very vehicles for his Body and Blood, and the means of our spiritual nourishment.

Holy Unction, the anointing of the sick, is likewise a vehicle of God's healing power. As we think of balm as a soothing medication, so have men always thought of unguents as symbols of healing. There is no magic involved in the offering up of petitions, nor yet in the hands which are laid upon the sick man's head. Neither is there any magic inherent in the oil with which the sign of the Cross is made upon a person's forehead in the sacramental rite of Holy Unction. That oil is blessed by the bishop of the diocese on Maundy Thursday. It is olive oil, used as an outward sign of the inward grace of healing.

As such, sacraments are not simply symbols, but actual vehicles and channels of Christ's continuing incarnation through his Body, the Church. Sacraments, then, are the literal means of his grace and the physical bearers of his Presence, whether that Presence be expressed via water, bread, wine, oil, or the hand of the priest touching the recipient in blessing.

The sacrament of the Holy Communion, for instance, is not merely a memorial feast. It has nothing in common with the act of placing a wreath on the tomb of the Unknown Soldier on Memorial Day, for instance. Nor are the consecrated elements of bread and wine merely symbols or reasonable facsimiles of reality. They then *are* the reality, under the outward guise of wine and bread.

This is not to insist that the Presence of Christ, invoked by the celebrant at Christ's own behest, changes the chemistry of the elements involved. The bread may still be the end result of the combined contributions of the wheat-growing farmer and of the dough-making baker; and the wine may still be the fermented fruit of some grape-grower's southern slope. But now it becomes all of these things, *plus the divine infusion of the Presence.* As the life of Jesus is the prime example of pure Spirit becoming flesh, so is the life of the Church the prime example of pure Spirit *continuing* to become flesh through sacramental channels.

Thus, the effectiveness of an individual healer's ministrations will depend upon the effectiveness of the healer himself. But the efficacy of a sacrament, thank God, does not rest upon the personality of the officiant. The faith of the priest can indeed be expected to be strong; and certainly the faith of the expectant patient will mount as the eagles. But the happy point is that the power of a sacrament does not thereby hang in the balance, as long as Faith with a capital "F" is somewhere present. And the fountain-head of the Faith reposes within the common tradition of the Holy Catholic Church as the Body of Christ throughout all history.

In *Healing: Human and Divine,* a symposium edited by Simon Doniger, Cyril Richardson writes:

Spiritual cures have certain marked characteristics which tend to recur in all the accounts, be they the records of Epidauros or of Lourdes. There is often a sudden acute pain which is directly related to the cure. There is the lack of a time factor. The healing is sudden, with no intervening period of convalescence. There is permanence. There is an ambiguous relation between faith and doubt, though faith in some form (of the patient, or the healer, or the Church) is invariably present. There is a general atmosphere of religious expectation. And finally, such cures are remarkably infrequent. About one per cent (or less) of the pilgrims to Lourdes receive bodily healing.[3]

Now, since Dr Richardson has presented us with six classical characteristics of spiritually induced cures within the narrow confines of one paragraph—and since each of the six is eminently worth noting individually—let's begin by listing them singly, so that each may make its proper impression, even upon the man who runs as he reads.

1. There is often a sudden acute pain which is directly related to the cure.

2. There is the lack of a time factor. The healing is sudden, with no intervening period of convalescence.

3. There is permanence.

4. There is an ambiguous relation between faith and doubt, though faith in some form (of the patient, or the healer, or the Church) is invariably present.

5. There is a general atmosphere of religious expectation.

6. And finally, such cures are remarkably infrequent.

It is important to note all of these characteristics; otherwise any spiritual healing will almost inevitably tend to be regarded as arbitrary miracle—in the wrong sense of that word—a complete break with the laws which govern the rest of the universe.

It is grossly unfair, however, to assume categorically that a miracle is an action which contravenes the order and law of the universe. It is significantly more reasonable to conclude that an event which upsets the expectancies of our neat little calculation may well be a lawful and orderly act of which we, with our limited knowledge, are as yet unaware. Because spiritual phenomena are often mysterious in their operations, it does not follow that they are therefore necessarily lawless.

As a matter of fact, it is quite the opposite which is more likely to be true. The abiding imponderables do not give up their secrets easily or casually to those who, having no time for other than pat conclusions, attempt to read as they run. According to the universally accepted precepts of the fifteenth century, the world was categorically flat—until a man named Christopher Columbus launched out into the deep. It took nothing short of such an act of faith to indicate that the final truth might lie somewhere else than where a prior acceptance had placed it.

So it is neither a by-passing of science, nor yet a criticism of science, to come with an open mind to the investigation of phenomena about which science is still ignorant, or which may lie forever outside the competence of the scientific approach. As more than one scientist has pointed out, it is a mistake to deny anything on the basis of laws which are themselves as yet scarcely understood.

Proof of the miraculous does not presuppose a collapse of old laws, but rather the operation of additional parts of the same old laws, *newly discovered*. It is patently not in the character of the Creator, as consistently revealed within the pages of the New Testament, ever to suspend the laws of his own creation. He doesn't suspend them. It is simply that he chooses, upon fitting occasions, to employ portions of the law of his orderly universe, of whose operations we as yet know little or nothing. As sharers in the completion of this still imperfect creation, we are constantly narrowing the gap between the known and the unknown. The lamp of knowledge burns ever brighter. But we continue, at the present hour, to fumble feebly through vast precincts of dark ignorance.

In his *Journey to Lourdes*, Dr. Carrel writes:

We still know almost nothing about the laws of nature and we are in constant danger, like primitive man, of thinking that the rumble of the thunder in the clouds is a manifestation of divine anger. . . . To say that something is not true without having first investigated the facts is to commit a grave scientific error. . . . Many people refuse to accept anything produced by the interplay of natural forces unless it fits in with facts long since established, described in books, and categorized more or less artificially within the scope of known theories. When a phenomenon too revolutionary to be fitted into the over-rigid framework of official science suddenly occurs, people deny it, or simply greet it with a smile. . . . An event or a fact is called supernatural when its cause is not known. . . . As Claude Bernard has said, we must try to break the fetters of philosophical and scientific systems as we would break the chains of intellectual slavery.

The laws of nature [he concludes] are still so thickly veiled in darkness, as far as we are concerned, that to limit our scope of investigations to the laws we now understand would mean a wilful narrowing of our horizons. . . . No research should be abandoned just because it presents difficulties, or because it is neglected or scorned by the learned men of that time.[4]

It is the province of the physician to try to rehabilitate the malfunctioning body, and of the surgeon to cut out the diseased tissue, or reset the shattered bone. This is not the prime function of the pastor. Neither is it within the competence of the priest to act as a psychiatrist. The priest is a counselor, not an analyst. True, the need for psychiatric help is great, and its practitioners are all too few. There are, admittedly, many instances where a good pastor can deal with the mildly neurotic situations; but for a clergyman to presume to deal with a psychotic condition is dangerous. A wise pastor quickly learns to know what he does not know—and he humbly abides by that knowledge. The handling of marked emotional disturbances is the psychiatrist's task, not the priest's.

It is the concern and conviction of the Church that first things should always be put first. Now if it be true, as we believe it is, that man is an indivisible trinity of body, mind, and spirit, then the Church is right in insisting that the spirit is of primary importance in that combination.

All three entities in this trinity are in constant interaction. It would naturally be impossible to tell where one starts and where another ends. On the elementary level, for example, we well know how thoroughly a badly functioning body can depress the spirit, and how much a radiantly healthy body can help lift that same spirit. Since the spirit, however, is of ultimate importance, the condition of both the mind and the body will depend upon the condition of a man's soul.

In short, the character of the whole personality will depend upon the condition of the soul. If the channel of communication between God and man has, for one reason or another, become clogged, it is the function of the Church as the Body of Christ to reopen this vital artery between the Creator and the created. For a man cannot function properly as a *whole* human being if his spirit is not a channel for the grace of God. The word *whole* means "hale," "healthy," and "to be saved" means "to be made whole."

The soul is so vital a part of the person that if the soul is sick, it will most likely follow that the man's emotional life will be disturbed. When a man's spiritual life has been clogged up, and the disaffection is not frankly faced and dealt with, the resulting paralysis is bound to put an unfair burden upon the nervous structure. Then it becomes necessary to call in the psychiatrist!

If, on the other hand, we refuse to admit that our emotions are out of control, and are foolishly afraid of the term "nervous breakdown," we may pretend that nothing is happening, when all the time the worst things in the world are happening to us, and unnecessarily.

However, we cannot go on this way forever. The spirit

and the emotions can take just so much, then something has to give. It is at this point often that the body is made to pay the bill for something which originally was not its fault at all. If the disease of the soul has not been faced and, for lack of having sought God's help through his Church, the spiritual illness becomes an emotional disturbance, it is easy to predict what the next step will be. An explosion of some sort will follow, and bodily illness is the result. This is why many physicians accept the hypothesis that the origin of many illnesses is to be found in something other than the body itself. The end may be in the body, but the origin was probably in another part of the interrelated trinity of body, mind, and spirit.

It is at this point that the ministry of healing comes in. Coming to the Church for the healing of a sick body, instead of for the cure of a sick soul, is certainly not putting first things first. For if the spirit were entirely well, then the body would be better equipped to resist disease. Yet almost every person who comes to the Church for healing comes for the cure, not of his soul, but of his body. This approach is understandable. Jesus called the body the "temple of the Spirit." Our Lord respected the body and, therefore, never treated it lightly. These temples of ours are often troublesome things, however, and even the best of them is destined to grind to a painful halt one day. Meanwhile, we do all we can to keep them functioning in reasonably good order.

Just as the chief goal of physical medicine is the healing of the body, so the immediate goal of psychosomatic medicine is the healing of the emotions—which, in turn, often leads to the healing of the body. But the ultimate goal of *spiritual* medicine (if one may use the term in the sense that "the Cross is the medicine of the world") is *the healing of the whole personality*. This kind of health includes the spirit, as well as the mind and the body.

Its springboard is the premise that the spirit, being immortal, is of infinitely greater value than sheer intellect or the outward framework of flesh and blood and bone. The tenant is of more value than the house he temporally inhabits. If the house, badly damaged by the storms of life, can be shored up and rebuilt, that is a consummation worth hoping and praying for. And Christians have always respected and enjoyed the body as the temple of the spirit. In the face of the ancient Greeks' disparagement of the flesh, the Church stoutly affirmed its value, climaxing this conviction about the body's worth in insisting upon the significance of Christ's resurrection from the dead.

A touching example of the proper attitude is shown in the following note from an inquirer:

This comes as a plea from an ignorant heart. I don't know a thing about spiritual healing, but I'd give anything to learn. My handicap is a tough one to bear, but I know that God understands the cause of it and the reason why I have it, even though it's still a dark mystery to me. Somehow I know that, through you, he can heal me. However, if he doesn't heal me immediately, maybe I can be taught to live with my trouble and to use it creatively.

There are many examples in hospital records which confirm the fact of remarkable bodily healings which from a strictly medical point of view are incomprehensible. From the Christian point of view, however, no case of a physical cure is ever more than a happy by-product of a search for a much deeper kind of healing. And unless that deeper type of healing comes first, or at least accompanies the physical cure, the latter has little chance of being permanent. Ten lepers pleaded with Jesus to be made whole and clean again. He promised them that they would indeed find themselves healed, and he then commanded them to present themselves to the priest. So the ten departed. Only one had the grace to return and offer his thanks. The nine were simply like many of the rest of us, taking the remarkable gifts of God for granted, and never thinking to return thanks for the outpouring of his countless blessings.

Actually, the lone leper who returned to make a stewardship of his gratitude was the only one of the ten who was thoroughly healed; he alone is termed "whole" by the Healer. His spirit had responded to Christ, with the result that his temple, having a happy tenant within it, was itself a happier place.

In this connection, we must remember the parable of the man who was delivered of a demon which was possessing him. The evil had been driven out, but it had not been replaced by something good. The end result was that seven worse devils came and took possession of the man.

Psychiatry understands the techniques required for driving out many of the demons which torture us because of our emotional traumas. But then, having ousted the demonic usurpers, I find it in my heart to wish that more psychiatrists would say, "Now I've done my part. The house of your soul is swept clean. At this point I can do no more. I have heard your confession on my couch. But

I cannot give you absolution. I cannot forgive you your sins. I cannot bring you the sacraments. I strongly advise you to go back to your Church. The next step for you is the most important one of all. And it takes place there with you in your parish." That which began in the psychiatrist's office should end at the Lord's altar.

In addition to Holy Unction and the Laying on of Hands and the Holy Communion, there is another sacrament generally associated with the ministry of healing, that of Penance. The Book of Common Prayer, in the office, the Visitation of the Sick, contains several incisive and carefully worded rubrics:

Here may the Minister inquire of the sick person . . . as to whether he repent him truly of his sins, and be in charity with all the world; exhorting him to forgive, from the bottom of his heart, all persons that have offended him; and if he hath offended any other, to ask them forgiveness; and where he hath done injury or wrong to any man, that he make amends to the uttermost of his power.

Then shall the sick person be moved to make a special confession of his sins, if he feel his conscience troubled with any matter; after which confession, on evidence of his repentance, the Minister shall assure him of God's mercy and forgiveness.

The healing intent of these instructions is crystal clear. The mere making of a generalized confession is not enough, especially *if he feels his conscience troubled with any matter*. And few, if any, of the saints themselves have gone long in life without feeling the gnawing pangs of a troubled conscience. Then a special confession shall be made, in which he freely forgives those who have offended him, thus wiping out any poisonous resentment from his heart.

He also humbly seeks the forgiveness of those whom *he* may have offended. And where he has wronged another man, he solemnly promises to make amends to the uttermost of his power. These are the demands of a classic penance! And it is only when they have been met that the penitent is absolved of his sins and assured thereby of God's forgiveness.

Since sin and sickness are often so closely allied—and in that order—these provisos have always been a traditional part of the life of the Church. It is thus by no mere accident that in the ordination service of the Episcopal Church these words appear:

Receive the Holy Ghost for the Office and Work of a Priest in the Church of God, now committed unto thee by the Imposition of our hands. Whose sins thou dost forgive, they are forgiven; and whose sins thou dost retain, they are retained. And be thou a faithful Dispenser of the Word of God, and of his holy Sacraments; In the Name of the Father, and of the Son, and of the Holy Ghost. Amen.

There are millions of men, reared in the Protestant tradition, who would be understandably uneasy at the screen of a confessional box, or even at the side of an altar rail. They would almost rather remain sick and keep the innermost thoughts of their hearts bottled up, than cleanse a troubled conscience in this fashion. These are the uncounted millions for whom the pastor's study is the fitting confessional, once they realize that God doesn't care *where* the floodgates break, as long as the stoppered heart is at long last gladly opened.

The central petition of the Christian religion is the Lord's Prayer, and the pivotal word of that prayer is a

iny conjunction. It is the word "as." "Forgive us our tres-
passes, *as* we forgive those who trespass against us." We
empower God to forgive us our shortcomings, only *as* we
forgive others theirs! Or, to put it another way, God's
forgiving power becomes fully effective in our relationship
to him and to our brothers *as* we first penitently seek his
forgiveness of our own sins, in terms of our having gladly
forgiven the sins of another against us.

I mention Absolution because, in the outline of "A
Good Visitation Office" suggested in that standard classic,
Liturgy and Worship,[5] it is the very first item mentioned.
It clears the way for the healing Spirit; indeed it is the
first step in the healing process itself. The order suggested
appeals to me greatly, for, even admitting the frequent
necessity of variations to meet personal needs, it includes
all the elements which I have observed to be constant. It
includes: Absolution, a selection of "confident and hopeful
prayers for the healing of soul and body," a brief instruction, the statement of the sick person's faith (the Apostles'
Creed), the administration of Holy Communion, "a period
of absolute silence with prayer for the descent of the Holy
Spirit," Unction, the Imposition of Hands, and silent prayer.
This is the method, but, remember, God alone is the cause!

This essay might well end with the words of the great
Dr. Trudeau of Saranac fame. This specialist in the cure
of tuberculosis was once asked what his goal was as a
Christian. His quiet answer should be the goal of all
Christians everywhere on the face of the earth:

"We are dedicated to a ministry which manages to heal
sometimes, to relieve often, and to comfort always."

THOMAS VAN B. BARRETT:

Joining Hands:
Holy Matrimony ❧   10.

There are various ways in which one might treat the subject of matrimony. If he had sufficient knowledge, one
might give a historical treatise on matrimony as practiced
by early Polynesians, middle period Egyptians, or the
Latter Day Saints of Utah. One might, I suppose, give an
essay on the development of Holy Matrimony in the
Church, or give you instructions on how to conduct a
wedding rehearsal when there are eight bridesmaids, two
flower girls, and a ring bearer to be dealt with, as well as
two mothers and a covey of great aunts. I am fairly certain
this would all be irrelevant to your deepest concerns. It
is the intent of these chapters to deal with a Christian
interpretation of the sacraments of the Church; and in this
chapter, what we are concerned with is not matrimony
but Holy Matrimony: marriage within the Church.

Christian marriage has much in common with any other

kind of marriage. It is a relationship of male and female which is both physical and spiritual, undertaken preferably on the basis of mutual love and understanding. Its cosmic purpose is the procreation of children in order to continue the species. Like any other type of marriage, Christian marriage has certain obligations to the state and society. It is also intensely personal and subjective. This twofold aspect is the source of much of the difficulty and conflict which at times surround love and marriage.

Christian marriage, however, has marks of distinction. It is a marriage: a union of two persons who are among the saints, members of the community of Christ, through which the Holy Spirit is at work. It is a union based upon the Christian understanding of the nature of man and the nature of God. In regard to man, this means we consider him created in God's image, with a portion of God's freedom, which through abuse leads man to sin, from which he needs to be redeemed. In regard to God, the Christian believes there is a divine order of creation, and that monogamy is a part of that order. It is good, not for economic reasons, nor because it is more convenient for society, but because every child is born of the union of two persons, and irrevocably related to those two other existences. The bond is indissoluble, and nothing can obliterate the uniqueness of this relationship. Furthermore, Christian marriage is founded on the belief that God has redeemed man through Christ, and will forever act toward man to sanctify him, to make him holy by his grace. A third mark of distinction about Christian marriage is that it is a union of man and woman lived in communion with the faithful, which is to say, it is a relationship which is to continue within the blessed community of the Church for the dura tion of life.

It seems clear to me that the service of Holy Matrimony in the Prayer Book supports these distinctive marks of a Christian marriage. It is a relationship "instituted of God," blessed by the Lord Christ, entered for the duration of life and *to be made holy* by the continuing power of the Holy Spirit, given through the sacrament itself, and abiding with those who have performed their solemn vows before God, and who live their lives in relationship to him.

The marriage service, and the customs surrounding it, were borrowed largely from the pagan Romans and given Christian meaning. The specially Christian ceremony added to the Roman marriage rites is the Nuptial Eucharist and the blessing by priest or bishop.[1]

I am not going further into these matters, but will try to discuss those aspects of matrimony in which all of us are most deeply involved: love, sex, the life of the Christian family. How can marriage increase and grow in richness and meaning; how can matrimony become holy?

The first necessity is a recovery of faith in God. Millions of people have for all practical purposes lost God in the clouds. He is a vague white blur, a secondary issue, a pious word used often with meager understanding. In the social and intellectual upheaval of this century, we have lost the simple, childlike trust in God's presence and activity; and in spite of church-going and professions of faith, our real trust is in other things: the bank, the stock market, the body beautiful, the home, the children, et cetera. We have been infected with the spurious humanism of the times, and accepted the dogma of "progress through science and technology." We have come to put our faith in the power of the human will; and like characters in a Faulkner novel, perversely keep saying we will cure ourselves, as we sink deeper and deeper into failure and impotence. We have a non-Christian interpretation of the condition of man.

I have spent most of my ministry around a college campus; and from the experience of talking with hundreds of students about love and marriage, sex and courting, I am convinced that much of the difficulty in making any progress at all toward a matrimony that is holy is linked to the fact that young men and women, like Willy Loman in *Death of a Salesman,* have a great many faulty ideas about everything important: love, suffering, sex, prayer, guilt, God—the very nature of earthly life, and man's destiny in the world. This is true of adults also. They have an image of life which is almost pure fiction; it coincides with the happy-ending movies and soap operas. Having lost faith in the hope of eternal life, modern man vainly tries to grasp happiness here on earth by means of economic security, will power, sexual adjustment, and positive thinking. Lacking a proper notion of *Christian love,* he thinks love is romantic passion; and when that fades with the years, he feels cheated and finds little to take its place or to supplement it.

Too many young people today believe that love is something that happens if and when you meet the one person in the world that is just for you; and that if you're lucky, you can hang onto it for a long while, particularly if the woman keeps her figure, or he keeps his hair. What fails to be understood is that love really is not something you have at the beginning of marriage and then lose; it is something to be won, struggled after, worked for, through all the years of trouble, sorrow, sickness, suffering, and occasional happiness, by giving up life, by sacrifice every step of the way. It has to be endured as well as enjoyed. It is a life of discipline, restraint, fidelity and duty, as well as a life of passion, ecstasy, and joy. And the love that emerges through this *labor* of matrimony is much more a "many-splendored thing" than the romantic infatuation at the beginning of marriage, which is in fact only an unknowing, instinctive kind of *eros,* romantic love, sufficient to risk the adventure of matrimony for a lifetime, in the faith that a deeper love and understanding may grow and come into flower.

From a Christian viewpoint, matrimony cannot become holy until man knows God and knows something about him. It is holy, in a sense, from the very outset at God's altar, where God gives his help to the man and woman entering into solemn contract with each other. Yet so subjective and so intimate is this relationship, so close to the depths of personality, that the Church may officially and legally perform a ceremony of Holy Matrimony which is not holy at all. It can, as someone said, join together an old man of seventy and a maiden of twenty-two who is thrust into the arrangement by parental influence, or for reasons of selfish aggrandizement, or whatever. The Church has blessed many an unholy alliance, because it performs a public function, and must do so, in what is fundamentally a mystical and hidden situation. This is one of the complexities of sacramental marriage, and can be one of the tragedies of human life.

What constitutes Holy Matrimony is the agreement of

two people in love to join together in wedlock for life's duration. The *ceremony* of Holy Matrimony, in a sense, publicly confirms a spiritual unity which has already come to pass—in the agreement already made in the privacy of two human souls—as baptism establishes an event that has already happened. The growth in holiness through the years must depend upon the relationship with their God of those who are joined together. If and when husband and wife come to know God, they will know that every man is Adam a sinner, and Job a sufferer, strung between two worlds, heaven and earth. In this earthly pilgrimage pain, guilt, love, fear, and death are indigenous. There is a sadness in the human heart as natural as stone is to earth, a restlessness not to be fulfilled even in the happiest marriage. Men have to learn again that they are failures at everything, including matrimony. They cannot make anything good or holy until they look upward and see the Cross rising out of the midst of evil—the condemnation of all pride and pretense of godliness—the sign that until men are ready to die to life, life is not given, nor love ever truly known.

Until we recover this kind of open-eyed faith so that we can look to the future with hope only in God, and beyond the future to eternal life, no ceremony in church will make a marriage holy; no partnership will ever free itself from selfish desire and ambition, unholy possessiveness and unmanly dependence. Without this faith we shall not have the strength to put aside "every root of bitterness, the desire of vain-glory, and the pride of life." (BCP, p. 598) We will not find the grace to make matrimony holy, nor be able to receive the grace given.

Next I wish to say a few things which have to do with the Christian attitude toward love and sex.

When my daughter was five or six years old, we drove one day to a neighboring town to see her grandparents. It was one of those halcyon days at the end of summer, when the world seems to stand still for a golden moment before rushing off into the riotous color of autumn, the kind of day a man or child might be struck with wonder and a touch of sadness. She asked the usual questions as we drove along: What's that and why? How long and when? After quite a pause she said, "I'd like to go to the end of the world; I bet it's an awful long way." "Why do you want to go?" I asked. "To see what it's like," she said.

All men wish to journey to the end of the world, to know the fullness of earthly existence, to drench themselves in whatever golden days there are. Men are filled with strange and contradictory desires. They search for a key to open the door to the hidden garden of meaning. They want food, shelter, security, liberty, a home on land, a place in the world. They want a mate, at least one other person with whom in the nakedness of the flesh and the spirit they can seek out the depths of human love.

In this longing, and in this finding—in man's experience of sexual love—is one of the signs that man is not destined for earth alone. For it seems to be profoundly true that this experience of sex (which man shares with the animal kingdom) is at its *best*, within the bond of love, an experience that is sacramental: which means flesh becomes the instrument of spirit. In sexual love at its noblest, man and woman enter into a union completely physical and yet supernatural, and they are bound together in the holiness of a love and beauty which is beyond good and evil; they achieve a mystical unity of being which reaches close to the meaning of love and of life. Yet the terrible thing about sex is that the actions which can be between lovers a sacred experience filled with spirit are, without love, actions of sheer animality, reducing men to a beastly level which ignores the divine gift of personality.

There may be people who enjoy sex without love, and who suffer little guilt from their adventures. They fall short of humanness; perhaps they are incapable of any real love, and respond only to the instinctual desires of natural man, in a nonpersonal, earth-bound sexuality. It is not their experience which provides the clue to the meaning of sexual love, but the experience of those who have known sex within the nimbus of love and, therefore, know it is too wonderful to be desecrated or adulterated through alliances without love.

Our society is saturated with sex; it has become a kind of obsession. But it is sex without wonder, sex as an end in itself, which confronts us in the movies, TV show, magazine rack, novel, and billboard advertising. Confined by puritanical attitudes for many years (which regarded sex as a somewhat naughty escapade even between married people), we have now become hypocritical about it and pretend publicly that it is of no great concern to us; while privately, or semiprivately, we furtively and slyly search for ways to express the natural desire that is in us.

We pretend to be chaste, monogamous, and disinterested in sexual things. We pretend that women's clothes, at seashore, in the office, or the ballroom, are designed to be attractive to other women. What nonsense! We pretend we are not interested in the sexy books, magazines, TV shows, and movies. But watch the respectable men hovering around the corner newsstands, afraid to buy, but sneaking a look or two. We pretend, as Philip Wylie said, that if we get a bunch of young soldiers into a USO canteen and let them play Ping-pong and have cocoa and cookies, they will abandon all desire to take Betty into the shrubs. Deep down, we know this is not true!

It would do us good to read *Green Mansions* again; to boycott the movies for a year, with their dreary innuendoes that people panting in a pseudopassion with unmussed hair have found happiness. Perhaps we should tear down the vulgar billboards filled with overblown cover girls and replace them with nudes by Rembrandt and Rubens, Botticelli and others, who looked with a keener and less lustful eye upon the fact of human bodies. One of the most beautiful verses in scripture that is relevant here is from Proverbs: "There be three things which are too wonderful for me, yea, four which I know not: The way of an eagle in the air; the way of a serpent upon a rock; the way of a ship in the midst of the sea; and the way of a man with a maid." (Proverbs 30:18, 19) It is the wonder of sex that we have lost. We treat sex as if it were a kind of hilarious hanky-panky, devoid of anything to do with God, spirit, splendor, and glory.

Our attitude toward sex is approaching the attitude of *Playboy* magazine. Sex is what we are here for; and it is completely embodied in the stupid looking pin-up girl with the swollen bosom, and the sly story of the fun that comes with infidelity. The problem is how we may re-educate people to some realistic understanding of the meaning of sex, of its mystical quality, its holiness within the bond of love, and its burdens of guilt outside of love; of the necessity for discipline and restraint of sexual desire, of the emptiness of sex when it is taken to be an end in itself, and the splendor of it when it is a sacrament of the spirit and an instrument of human love and the desire to journey to the end of the world.

It is the Christian's belief that no earthly experience can be rich and complete unless it is entered into in the faith that God is the author of all experience, the giver of all gifts. But sex does not gain its highest meaning, nor does it take its proper place in man's life, until it is accepted as a gift of God to be treated sacramentally by spiritual as well as physical creatures, whose destinies lie beyond the earth.

It is when sexual love is surrounded by divine love that it begins to be raised up out of selfish need, possessiveness, animal desire, and the dark waters of guilt into the mystical union of man and woman. In this experience there is a wonder and a new dimension of holiness given by the grace of God to those who, in the bond of love, know themselves to be both mortal and immortal.

While sex between lovers can be a beautiful and holy thing, the Church is correct in its loyalty to the ideal that sexual love at its noblest is discovered by those who have entered into the indissoluble contract of marriage. It is unconditional offering of self to self for life together, with all its sorrows and difficulties, joy and gladness, "for richer for poorer, in sickness and in health," which is essential for that highest understanding of the significance and purpose of sexual love.

It is through the sharing of every experience in marriage that sexual love achieves its deepest meaning; so that at the end of life it is seen as but one instrument for the expression of a love molded also by companionship, affection, reverence, loyalty, and unselfish caring devotion within the *agape*, the forgiving and completely un-needing love of God.

Christians then will seek to find within marriage the fullness of sexual experience, and will seek to find it with a wholesome and unselfish abandon, knowing it to be the gift of God; believing that within it there may be found a love not only human but divine, an awareness of the dignity of human personality lifted from nature to supernature by the enveloping love of God.

Yet one ought to end any such discussion with words such as these of Emil Brunner:

Even the Christian and the Christian moralist stand baffled and helpless before many of the problems of marriage . . . so long as marriage exists there will be insoluble problems; so long as man lives in this flesh he will never finally solve the problem of his sex nature. Even in the ethic of marriage the final word must be: to live on the Divine forgiveness.[2]

The final matter I wish to speak about is the life of the Christian family, which is again to ask the question: In what ways can our matrimony become holy—a relationship which exists not for itself nor in itself but is penetrated and continually strengthened by the Holy Spirit?

The cosmic purpose of marriage is the procreation of children, though this is not the subjective purpose, not the sole purpose. Because of this cosmic purpose I assume the Christian believes that if it be God's grace, every

Christian marriage looks forward to the "gift and heritage of children." What I have to say takes for granted that a Christian home will preferably be a home with children, even if some of them have to be adopted. And I will divide what I have to say in two parts: religion in the home, and religion in the Church.

When we speak of religion in the home we often make a mistake. We are inclined toward the idea that religion is an ecclesiastical kind of thing—a churchly affair—and so we introduce religion into the home along strictly church lines, something made up out of formal prayers, corner altars, and Bible pictures. We often fail to make clear how ubiquitous God is. Archbishop William Temple once said, "It is a mistake to think that God is exculsively or even primarily interested in religion." God is interested in life; he is involved, or would like to be involved, with many activities and experiences of every home. When we think of him as being limited to churchly activities, we overlook the possibilities of spiritual reality in the common everyday affairs of life.

In distant days almost every family was engaged in cooperative labor. In pastoral, rural, small town, and even seafaring communities it was not unusual for all members of a family to share in some common enterprise. This kind of family enterprise is rapidly disappearing. Today a father may work fifty miles or more from home, and his work may be so specialized in its nature that nobody in the family understands exactly what he does. Very often the mother works, fifty miles in another direction, at a different kind of labor. This means that it is difficult for father or mother or both to express to each other and to children the ambitions, failures, successes, or frustrations of the daily work.

"Pop" is out of the house all day and generally a nincompoop about the machine shop of the modern home, so it is hard for him to understand the enthusiasm of his wife about her daily triumphs over the perversity of Venetian blinds, washing machine, garbage disposal and dishwasher, furnace fan, and automatic oven. And it is even more difficult for her to comprehend the frustrations of a job so specialized that he is the only one of five hundred employees that can do it.

This separateness of work in the modern family has obvious disadvantages. Six people come home at night from various unrelated tasks and carry their separateness in six different rooms, with six different TV sets tuned to six different channels. A common work once contributed to the unity of the home; now that this element has vanished, new means of unification have to be discovered.

Some families have found a new sense of the unifying influence of work in some corporate avocation. The business of building a patio, a garden, a boat in the garage, a hi-fi set, or what not, has provided some modern families with a means of mutual understanding. Various crafts and hobbies, many of which are discovered to relate to each other, sometimes enable families to pool their various talents, and to learn something of communal enterprise; to rediscover that the holy spirit of affection and sacrifice and understanding comes in the process of working together, whether it be for money or for fun.

Families should also find ways of playing together. The fruits and by-products of family recreation in the old-fashioned home most of us have lost in the process of becoming a spectator people. In my childhood we had to make our own amusements. We made music together, played checkers, hearts, Guggenheim, croquet, or whatever. Certain games were reserved for certain days, or occasions or seasons, and they were fitted with some care into the patterns of our family life, like the "hymn sing" on Sunday evening, with the potato salad that preceded it, and the inevitable paper and pencil game that followed it. A family learns of affection, forbearance, laughter, and loyalty not so much from books as from shared experience. When a family discovers ways to work and play together, and maintains these activities as long as possible through the years, it begins to learn of God's presence in daily life; to know that God does not restrict his love toward us to a Sunday morning revelation, but mysteriously and subtly floods our lives, so that we come to be aware of his presence when we are at work together in a garden, or playing with children in the autumn leaves, or singing songs around a piano, or shouting wildly at a Little League ball game; we learn to rejoice that he comes to be with us in work and play, in the secular activities as well as the sacred; for actually he makes no great distinction between the two. When we allow him entrance, his Holy Spirit fills up our daily lives.

I have always been grateful to my parents that they took time to emphasize in the home the great days and seasons of the Church Year. Certain fairly fixed rituals were performed from year to year at Christmas, Thanksgiving, Easter, New Year's Day, which have left me with cherished memories, and have made these days more sacred, even though some of the rituals were not particularly ecclesiastical. And even the secular holidays, so-called, were celebrated in our family with some degree of uniformity of tradition.

We observed these nonreligious days religiously; they were home days, and we anticipated each one with some excitement, looking forward to each because over the years they had become sources of rich and often holy experience, as we learned from them something of family discipline, and mutual friendship and joy.

For example, the Fourth of July in my family was a great day. We were not allowed to shoot off any firecrackers until the morning of the day itself; and then we had one long rousing cannonade of cracker, cap, candle, and skyrocket, which began at six in the morning and ended at some dreadful hour of the night. My father had an old muzzle-loading cannon, forged by my grandfather. It made a boom which could be heard all the way from Cold Spring Harbor, Long Island, to New London, Connecticut. Father alone was man enough to fire it. He did so about four times a day. We kids stuffed cotton in our ears; my mother, who was anti-cannon, retreated to the kitchen, and the collie went under the bed in the guest room. When that cannon went off with a resounding boom that echoed proudly down the bay, and when the smoke arose thick and blue over the garden, we knew that we were independent! Liberty was our birthright.

It was a very secular day, but it had sacred overtones. Considering the punk shared, the sympathy offered when a finger was burned, the firecrackers borrowed and loaned and returned; considering that beneath the childish noise there was a meaning conveyed to us of a time when men rose up in dignity and courage to become free and responsible men of a new country; there was a sacredness about the day as well as a secularness. As though a man might say: "Surely God is in this place though I knew it not." (cf. Genesis 28:16) For all I know, God may have enjoyed the noise of the cannon and cried out, "Hurrah!"; for the cannon was aimed at no one; only at the tree tops and the sky beyond; a noisy shout in praise of valor and the thirst of a human spirit after liberty!

In regard to specific religious activities in the home, we ought at least to have grace before meals. We ought to have family prayers, but I am not sure we have much chance, given the tempo and complexity of modern life, to restore family prayer to its rightful place. Children catch buses, fathers catch trains, people stay up later and rise later and attend more meetings, and are more hurried, which is unfortunate. Prayers, except by children at bedtime (most innocent praying for others) and by parents too, individually at least, will not come back into popular custom until people increase much in piety, or until the condition of the culture changes.

But there are things that can and should be done individually: times of Bible reading, or devotional reading for adults and children. If you have trouble understanding the Bible, get a picture book, or some proper guide, or one of the new colloquial translations.

And there is another way of bringing religion into the home, though less formal and ecclesiastical, through religious art and music, which to many Christian homes have neglected. I am not speaking of the Sunday School art, or sentimental pictures of little boys in a garden with Jesus, or the prints of Gothic cathedrals, but of the excellent and imaginative pictures of past and present which can be purchased in fine reproductions and which have something to do with the revelation of God in beauty and in truth to the sons of men. Children ought to grow up in homes where the great and noble thoughts of Christian men and women surround them in art as well as literature and music. Instead of little Jennie and the bluebird hanging over the crib, put on the wall some classic of Leonardo or Giotto, or El Greco, Cezanne, Rouault, or even those more secular artists, who are competent, perceptive, and look with wonder and delight upon God's created world. For a painting of wheat fields by Van Gogh, or peasants dancing in a street by Breughel may have more religion than the picture of Jesus meek and mild, drawn by the same second-rate hack who draws Jennie with the windblown skirt for the tradesmen's calendars.

This applies to music also. Most families no longer make their own music. On TV and radio we hear two types: jazz and the popular classics, once in a while a sentimental gospel hymn. But most of us have record players, and we might well surround our children, and ourselves, with a reasonable portion of church music. Think of the large library of magnificent religious symphonies, oratorios, cantatas, from Bach and Handel to Hindemith, Paul Creston, and Honegger. Let your family hear some of the music which speaks of man's spiritual experience, and otherworldly aspiration, music which is composed and performed by Christians making their offering of praise to the Lord.

Through all these things, work, play, music, art, the

observance of special days and seasons, the religious life of a home is nourished. These are all avenues of the Holy Spirit, for in these family celebrations and rituals which parents and children take time to prepare and undertake, God cannot be far off. In the common tasks and uncommon occasions God comes if we let him; and through the shared joys and the shared sorrows, we become aware of his presence and the strength and gladness it brings. In homes where these activities and events go on, matrimony is on its way to becoming holy: a home where every sadness is relieved by faith, every sin by forgiveness, and every evil by love.

And what beyond this is required in the home? Allegiance, endurance, fidelity; how many things: the long wait through the night beside the sick child; the prayerful walking through the hospital corridors, waiting, waiting for the healing, the cry of pain, the birth of a son; the daily faithfulness to the chores of the home and the cares of the family; the keeping of silence through endless annoyances, when the selfish will wants to speak out in hurt pride or the desire to dominate; the endurance of all the jarring little traits and habits and gestures and mannerisms that grow in all of us through the years; the tenderness when we want to be gruff, and the steadfastness when we want to run away and escape from the demanding decision or the unpleasant situation; the giving up, time after time, year after year, of what *I* want to do, in order that man and wife and family together may grow in wisdom and in wholesomeness of spirit; the sometimes almost intolerable claims upon the self that have to be accepted; the cheerful words that have to be spoken in place of the words of gloom and bitterness that come rushing to the lips. Love has to be worked for, wept for, struggled for.

And when it all seems too hard and to demand too much; when it seems as though we can do nothing but try to escape, then, for the Christian, does it not mean the recollection that this is what he came into the world to do? To marry, and to raise a family, and to know how much sacrifice must be made before love lays bare its meaning; to go to the end of the world with one other person as imperfect as all persons are imperfect, working and striving for the fullness of each love in its season, romance, passion, friendship and companionship, lover's love, parent's love, brother love, divine love, seeking the mystical union that can come to those whose lives are built in love and crowned with the love of God.

Finally, as I said at the beginning, Christian marriage is marriage within the community of Christians, and must be continued within that community if it is to become holy. We need not only a continuing experience of God's spirit in our daily life; we need a continuing experience with other Christians. There is no vital understanding of God apart from his church, nor any full experience of his most holy presence apart from this community of faithful believers.

The Church is like a roadside stand along life's highway: a place of rest and refreshment where the soul is stilled, and the heart and mind refilled by the waters of life. The Church is the information bureau where we learn the detours that must be avoided, and which highways are filled with beauty. *Holy* Matrimony is marriage which stays close to Christian truth, a union between two persons who return again and again to this place of guidance to read the signs that are posted by the saints and prophets of old, in order to know with clarity which way to go.

The Church is a place of companionship where Christians gather in fellowship in the unity of the spirit to strengthen and encourage one another; to forgive and to be forgiven; to be reinforced for life on the open road in the non-Christian world.

Matrimony cannot achieve holiness without the Church. The home is not enough, though God may invade the home each day. It is essential to return continually into the midst of the people of God, into the midst of this company of Christ, and to know his coming in the power of the spirit into this small, steadfast little Kingdom.

Through the habitual participation in the Church's liturgies; through prayer, sermon, *sacrament,* our perceptions are sharpened, our knowledge of God deepened, our knowledge of ourselves clarified; and all our drained and selfish lives are forgiven, rededicated, made more loving. The more we come to know God amongst his followers, the more often we see his footsteps along the paths of our daily life, even in places where we did not expect to find him. God comes to visit in the homes of those who have discovered him before his altar.

Marriage is not a special privilege of Christians. What *we* are concerned with is Christian marriage, between members of the blessed community in Christ. For us marriage is an indissoluble bond entered into without condition or reservation, undertaken for the duration of life, with an open readiness to face and accept every risk, every danger involved.

There may be times when in spite of the solemn contract of the vows, and in spite of the most honest intentions, it is better to sever the marriage by divorce than to continue in lovelessness and sheer endurance, after the real qualities of marriage have been lost; after the unity has become simply a legal or churchly word. But one of the evils of the time is that too many people enter marriage with a mental reservation that an escape from its difficulties can be found in divorce; and too many tend to flee their obligations and to forget their vows at the first few signs of strain and stress. For too many, divorce is a false solution to a marriage problem. But the Christian will hold to the ideal; and work valiantly and patiently toward it, believing God can bring love and understanding into a relationship when humans fail. Christian marriage is one in which both partners recognize at the beginning that all men fail, and must always throw themselves upon God's forgiveness.

Christian men and women are those who admit that human love, however wonderful, is mixed with pride and jealousy and possessiveness. They know all the loves of earth need to be offered up to God to be purified by his grace. They know the life of matrimony requires the everlasting and continuing sacrifice of self. And this is not possible to attain except when men and women are overshadowed by the wings of the Lord, and all the sadness, struggle, and joy of marriage are transposed to a new key by his loving kindness.

Partners in a Christian marriage know they have a goal beyond the goal of those who are not Christian—not sex, nor security, nor contentment, nor any earthly happiness, all of which are by-products of the great adventure. The end of marriage for a Christian is eternal life within the family of God. There the frail and partial unities of *this* world come to fulfillment. In this Christian hope, man and woman can best achieve a real and abiding marriage. Holy Matrimony for us is a joining of hands in great humility and very great faith, with the desire to make the journey to the end of the world together in mutual trust, reverence, devotion, love, and courage, believing that God will give his help unto the end of life, and bring us into that eternal Kingdom where we may stand with all our earthly love perfected by his presence and, in the company of the saints, give praise to him.

EDWARD N. WEST:

Apostolic Hands:
Holy Order ❧ 11.

Long established principles of action are, generally, only thought through as to their implications when opposition challenges their whole establishment. So, for example, the common assumption of New Testament days that the world would soon end had to be thought through in terms of fiscal application only when certain Christians gave up their jobs and refused to do any more work. St. Paul's practical mind supplied an immediate and effective answer—*If they won't work, don't feed them!* In the same manner, the normal growth and development of the Church's Order came to be thought through only when schism and heresy attacked its fundamental assumption— the fundamental assumption being that Christ had put orders in the Church in order to keep the Church in order. All difficulties about Apostolic Succession arise only when people, either within or without the boundaries of the historic Church, attempt to consider Holy Orders as things apart from the sacred Body they were meant to serve. To assume that bishops, priests, or deacons have either authority or spiritual power apart from the Church is to invest orders with the nature of magic. To assume that the "priesthood of all believers" implies that all Christians are basically in Holy Orders and, that they just choose out several to act as traffic officers, is to miss completely the function of the Apostles in the early Church and to ignore the endowment of the Spirit with which the Church is instinct. Firminger, in his brilliant essay on the Ordinal, states the whole matter superbly:

That which is bestowed on an ordinand by Ordination is not merely something which distinguishes him from the laity on the one hand, or from other ministers in an hierarchy on the other; nor is it even a power—a personal property of his own—of performing this or that service or office. By the laying on of hands with prayer, the ordinand receives, or is admitted into, that endowment of the Holy Spirit which (1) is the extension throughout the ages of Christ's gift to his Apostles, and (2) is nothing else but the abiding presence and power of him whose office it is to cleanse, sanctify, illumine and sustain. The minister can do nothing apart from the operation of the Holy Spirit, who takes of the things of Christ and presents them to the Church (John 16:15). Apart from the operation of the Giver of life, all sacraments are of necessity null and void. Through the presence and power of the Holy Spirit, the one abiding Priest employs his chosen earthly minister as his living instrument; but it is he himself who baptizes, confirms, consecrates the Eucharistic elements, absolves the penitent, ordains and admits men as his ministers, joins hands in Christian wedlock, and strengthens the sick.[1]

One may insist that in the early Church it was possible for prophets to say the prayers at the communion service. One may note that in the Pastoral Epistles the words *bishop* and *presbyter* (elder) are often used almost interchangeably, and one may admit quite honestly that the first deacon, St. Stephen, was most obviously not put to death for being kind to old ladies and orphans. One may recognize that the term *bishop* and the term *presbyter* are in early Latin writings regarded as synonymous, but the fact still remains that the statement in the preface to the Ordinal is undeniable: "from the Apostles' time there have been these Orders of Ministers in Christ's Church—Bishops, Priests, and Deacons." (BCP, p. 529)

Professor John Knox, in his brilliant book, *The Early Church and the Coming Great Church,* points out the exact situation in several brilliant paragraphs:

We have observed Paul's acknowledgment of the authority of the apostle and his insistence upon the importance of that authority to the order and unity of the church. It is interesting to note how clearly, repeatedly, and emphatically the Gospels strike this same note. One is likely to think first of such texts as 'I will give you the keys of the kingdom of heaven . . .' (Matt. 16:19) or 'Whatever you bind on earth shall be bound in heaven, and whatever you loose on earth shall be loosed in heaven.' (Matt. 18:18; compare John 20:20-23.) But to passages of this kind must be added the several in which the authority vested in the disciples is referred to in connection with Jesus' choice and commissioning of them, as, for example, 'He . . . sent (them) out to preach and have authority to cast out demons' (Mark 3:14-15; compare Mark 6:7; Matt. 9:37-10:2; Luke 6:12-13; 9:1-2, 6; John 6:70; 15:16). Equally impressive are the directions Jesus gives his disciples when he sends them out (see Matt. 10:5-15 and Luke 10:2-12), culminating in such sweeping assurances as 'He who receives you receives me, and he who receives me receives him who sent me' (Matt. 10:40), or 'He who hears you hears me, and he who rejects me rejects him who sent me' (Luke 10:16), or (in a somewhat different context) 'As thou didst send me into the world, so I have sent them into the world' (John 17:18; compare 13; 18-20). . . .

It can be argued that for Jesus his disciples constituted, not officials of the church, but the community itself; and that such words of his as have just been quoted were intended to confer authority on the whole church, not on the apostles as such. The whole church was 'sent.' But it is much easier to make this point about Jesus' original intention (assuming the authenticity of the words themselves) than about the way the words were understood in the primitive church; and we must keep in mind that it is understanding with which we are at present really concerned. Could Luke 22:28-30 (compare Matt. 19:28), 'You are those who have continued with me in my trials; as my Father appointed a kingdom for me, so do I appoint for you that you may eat and drink at my table in my kingdom, and sit on thrones judging the twelve tribes of Israel'—could such a passage have been understood, say in A.D. 80, as not being addressed to the twelve apostles in their official capacity? . . .

Concerning Luke-Acts, and especially the Acts section. . . . No one will question that its way of telling the story of primitive Christianity is affected in every part by its interest in promoting the unity of the contemporary church. Christians everywhere belong to the true Israel, the covenant people of God. To set forth this character of Christianity as successor to, indeed the continuation of, the Hebrew-Jewish religious community (and therefore a corporate unity) is perhaps the primary objective of Luke-Acts. We have interpreted Ephesians and the first Pauline letter collection as being, under one aspect at least, an effort to present Paul as an ecumenical church leader; Acts might be described, also under one aspect, as another effort of the same kind. In the collected letters Paul is allowed to speak for himself, for the most part; in Acts an interpreter speaks for him. But in both cases Paul speaks to the whole church and for the sake of the whole church. The author of Acts does his best to present a convincing picture of an early church at peace with itself, united in a common order and gladly acknowledging the authority of the Jerusalem authorities, whether 'the apostles and the elders' (15:6) or 'James . . . and all the elders' (21:18). One does not need to doubt his sincerity in order to recognize that he would probably not have presented the primitive situation, just as he did, or indeed have seen it so, if he had not been concerned to help unify and consolidate the church in his own time.[2]

If we are to understand what these offices have come to mean in the Church, it is essential that we make some effort to see them first in their New Testament context. The power to bind and loose, which came to have such grim associations in the days of the Inquisition, was not a new sort of thing dreamed up by the early Church and projected back into the mouth of Christ. In our Lord's own day, common Rabbinic exegesis made it clear that "the sound of the trumpet binds, and the sound of the trumpet looses." Indeed this was and is the commonly accepted explanation of the blowing of the shophar on the Hebrew Day of Atonement. It was then, and is now, impossible to have any religious organization competent to maintain its own ordered life without the power to eject or place under discipline those who are voiding its fundamental reason for existence. A religious organization can never rightly have coercive power. Indeed, all human history points up the fact that it is suicidal for any religious body to rely on the coercive powers of the state to preserve that religious body's own inner harmony. As Lea pointed out, the tragedy of the Inquisition is not the few thousands tortured and killed, but, rather, the permanent mark it has

left on the life and character of Spain.[3] (We should note
that the same can and must be said of every other similar
institution, regardless of the particular communion or
church which fostered it.) The elders, or presbyters, of
Israel had both the authority and responsibility to see that
the Law of God was kept. They had the power of binding
and loosing and exercised it freely. The Christian family, of
necessity, had the same power; thus the seemingly dread
charge to the Apostles would in New Testament days be
regarded as something quite normal to family life. Obviously, there was a difference in the binding and loosing
done in the Christian community, since it was *love* rather
than *law* which was to be administered; but it was still the
ancient method though differently applied. Indeed, we
often miss the point of this binding and loosing by assuming that it was superior to the receipt of the Holy Ghost
and the commission to preach the gospel, heal the sick,
and in general, be living witnesses to a living Lord. It is
only when one recognizes that the holy Mysteries of the
Christian's holy communion with his living Lord were the
absolute center of his devotional life, that the power of
binding and loosing, or including or excluding people at
the Holy Table, starts to make its full sense. The cautionary
rubrics at the end of the communion service are but a
Byzantine canonical summary of the application of the
powers of excommunication, and it will be noted that these
powers rest in the priest only by delegation. A priest,
exercising any one of them must promptly report the matter
to the Bishop, who in turn can bind or loose the particular
offense. And the reason for this is that the bishops as over-
seers of the early Church were regarded not only as ad-

ministrative officials but as men of responsible authority chosen to have the oversight of Christ's flock with the obligation of feeding that flock.

The exact New Testament references are: ". . . the flock, over which the Holy Ghost hath made you Bishops, to feed the Church of God . . ." (Acts 20:28) "The Shepherd and Bishop of your souls . . ." (I Peter 2:25) The three-fold restoration of Peter in each instance relates love of the Lord with responsibility for *feeding* the Lord's sheep. (cf. St. John 21:1-7.)

It is in this very insistence on the bishop as one who sees that the flock of Christ is fed that we discover all the underlying and essential meaning of Apostolic Succession. The Apostles, as the very word implies, were men *sent* forth by Jesus Christ, who in turn had been *sent* by the Father. It is not really the burden of the Church to prove that the Lord commissioned and sent forth men by the laying on of hands; rather, in view of the universal practice of Israel in which the laying on of hands was used for blessing, for healing the sick, for absolving from sin, and for ordaining Israel's elders, the burden of proof lies on anyone who would attempt to prove that it was done any other way. Even in its late and Greek context, the Lucan account of the Ascension (at the end of the Gospel) certainly assumes the use of the Lord's hands in the final commissioning. That the Apostolic College (the Twelve) in turn commissioned and *sent forth* men by the power of the Holy Spirit inherent in the Church is not even debatable. The real problem lies rather in the process whereby the official ministry gradually became omnicompetent, and, in doing so, both absorbed and ended the charismatic ministries prevalent in the early Church.

Parenthetically, a word is in order about these charismatic ministries, since there is at this moment a considerable revival of them on the West coast of this country. In the early Church, *speaking with tongues* was regarded as a regular, if not always happy, adjunct of religious enthusiasm. St. Paul certainly regarded it as one of the functions of religious life, but not necessarily as one of the ministries in the sense of its being a regularly appointed ecclesiastical office. By the time St. Luke is writing, he assumes that *speaking with tongues* meant speaking with other *human* tongues; hence his moving but somewhat oversimplified picture of Pentecost. *Prophets,* however, lingered on in the Church much longer, and as late as the second century certain backwoods areas would still have been used to prophets doing the chief amount of public praying in church. As over against this, it is to be noted that the *episcopos* (overseer or president) was the continuing officer who presided at the Christian Mysteries, whether he said the prayers or not. He it was who determined who could and who could not partake of these Mysteries; he it was who acted as the chief public witness to the knowledge of a risen Lord in the Breaking of Bread. To be a Christian, one had to be in communion with him, and he in turn, to be recognized as a Christian, had to be in communion with his fellow *episcopoi* throughout his immediate province; whereas the charismatic ministry by its very nature needed no official admission to that status.

The very order of the Church required that its regular

ministers should be duly *sent* forth by men who in turn had themselves been duly *sent* forth. When we are talking about Apostolic Succession, we are talking first and foremost about liturgical succession—the ministry of those who have, from the Apostles' days, and by the Apostles' own commissioning, had the public oversight of the Church for the purpose of seeing to it that the flock was *fed*. The feeding of the flock of Christ is the *public work* of the Church, and *public work* is exactly what the word liturgy means. In the strictest historic terms, you could have done without presbyters or deacons at any time, but you could never at any time have done without the *episcopoi*.

It is necessary for me to press this point because in our Western way, we are inclined to think that a man is made a deacon, and then some more Holy Ghost is added and he is made a priest; and, other things being equal, even more Holy Ghost is added and he is made a bishop. This is exactly the reverse of the procedure. The bishop delegates a portion of his ministerial responsibility to a man and makes him a deacon. A bishop delegates a portion of his pastoral responsibility to a man and makes him a priest, but the bishop reserves certain functions to himself such as Confirmation (or the blessing of the Chrism to be used for it), Ordination, and the commutation of public penance. All things start from the top rather than from the bottom; because, even above and beyond the bishop, is the plenitude of the Spirit which enables him, in a covenanted arrangement, to serve the flock of Christ. It is essential at this point to be reminded that things really do come from the top, as *Liturgy and Worship* notes:

. . . in the Orthodox prayer for the ordination of a deacon, the Bishop says: 'it is not by the laying on of my hands, but by the watchfulness of thy rich mercies that grace is given to thy chosen men.' With this thought the English 'King's Book' of 1543 concurs. 'Priests and bishops, although in the execution of their office and administration they do use and exercise the power and authority of God committed unto them, yet they be not the principal causes, nor the sufficient, or of themselves the efficient causes or givers of grace, or any spiritual gift which proceedeth and is given by God by his word and sacraments; but God is the only principal, sufficient and perfect cause of all the efficacy of his word and sacrament; and by his only power, grace and benefits it is that we receive the Holy Ghost, and by his graces, by the office and administration of the same priests and bishops; and the said priests and bishops are but only as officers to execute and minister with their hands and tongues the outward and corporal things wherein God worketh and giveth grace in word, according to his pact and covenant made with and to his espouse the Church.' [4]

In liturgical terms, the hardest thing to account for is not how the *overseer* of the New Testament became the monarchical *bishop* of the second century; but, rather, how the *presbyters* of the New Testament (the elders of the community, in Jewish terms) turned into *priests*. The system of elders was of long standing in Israel, dating, traditionally, from the appointment of the seventy elders in the wilderness, and the ordination of Joshua. Every Jewish community had elders, ordained by members of their own collegium, who had responsibility for the whole carrying on of religion in the synagogue. It was in many ways a congregationalist system, the *minister* being employed by the elders, and the *ruler* of the synagogue being a layman.

In the Christian community, the elders functioned much like a sort of consecrated vestry. Being senior and substantial men, they were responsible for the meeting place and for the collection of funds. There is a liturgical remain of their self-perpetuating ordination in the fact that in our own day priests join with the bishop in the laying on of hands when a man is ordained to the priesthood. In modern terms, this certainly serves to symbolize the ordinand's admission to the presbyteral college. As it stands now, *in strictly liturgical terms,* the ordinand is made both an elder and a priest, in that he is admitted, by the laying on of the presbyters' hands, to an order with rights of its own; but he is also, by the bishop's prayer and action, admitted into that specific delegation of the bishop's pastoral responsibility, which has since the second century come to be known as the priesthood.

The New Testament knows nothing of the title of priest, save as applied to our Lord himself, when the writer of Hebrews (5:6) refers to him as a priest after the order of Melchizedek who became our great high priest. It is not until the Clementine epistles that the full sacerdotal terminology of the Old Testament comes to be applied to the ministry of the Christian Church. It is, however, to be recognized that even this was a further attempt to think through Christ's sacrificial and high priestly function as prefigured by the Old Testament, rather than as a conscious attempt to exalt the Christian ministry. By the time of the great Ignatius of Antioch there is complete and reliable evidence of the existence of bishops in the patristic sense of that word. The *overseer* of New Testament days is now the single-ruling, or monarchical, bishop.

Whereas Clement of Rome was interested in bishops and deacons (overseers and ministers) chiefly because they were appointed by the Apostles for the care of the Church (this was about the year 95), Ignatius assumes that the bishop is both the criterion of orthodoxy, and the test of all sound and valid communion with God and with one's fellow Christians (this, by the year 112).

Admittedly, whenever Tertullian speaks well of anything, the instinct of all healthy minds is to suspect that there must be something wrong with it. It is, however, in spite of this, important to note that, writing in about the year 200, he could present the following statements as the common presuppositions of his time:

. . . The Apostles first bore witness to the faith of Christ Jesus through Judaea; they founded churches there, and then went out into the world and preached to the nations the same doctrine of the same faith. They likewise founded churches in every city, from which the other churches thereafter derived the shoot of faith and the seeds of doctrine—yea, and are still deriving them in order to become churches. It is through this that these churches are themselves apostolic, in that they are the offspring of apostolic churches. Every kind of thing must needs be classed in accordance with its origin. And so the churches, many and great as they may be, are really the one Primitive Church issuing from the Apostles, which is their source. So all are primitive and all apostolic, while all are one. And this unity is proved by the peace they share, by their title of brotherhood, by their contract of hospitality; for these privileges have but one ground, the one tradition of the same revelation (*sacramentum*).

But if any of these (heresies) are bold enough to insert themselves into the Apostolic age, in order to seem to have been handed down from the Apostles because they existed under the Apostles, we can say: Let them then produce the origins of their churches; let them unroll the list of their bishops, an unbroken

succession from the beginning so that that first bishop had as his
precursor and the source of his authority one of the Apostles or
one of the apostolic men who, though not an Apostle, continued
with the Apostles. This is how the apostolic churches report their
origins; thus the church of the Smyrnaeans relates that Polycarp
was appointed by John, the church of Rome that Clement was
ordained by Peter. . . .[5]

It was inevitable that so lofty a concept of the office
of a bishop should now and then be frustrated by the in-
adequacy of the man chosen for that position. Writing
just about 200 years later, Gregory of Nyssa could say,

Accordingly it would well become you to entertain thoughts
that shall not fall below the height of the blessings that now
are yours, but to raise your enthusiasm in the work before you
to the height of the magnificence of your city, that you may find
such a one to preside over the laity as will prove himself not
unworthy of you. For it is disgraceful, brethren, and utterly
monstrous, that while no one ever becomes a pilot unless he is
skilled in navigation, he who sits at the helm of the Church
should not know how to bring the souls of those who sail with
him safe into the haven of God. How many wrecks of Churches,
men and all, have ere now taken place by the inexperience of
their heads! Who can reckon what disasters might not have been
avoided, had there been aught of the pilot's skill in those who
had command? Nay, we entrust iron, to make vessels with, not
to those who know nothing about the matter, but to those who
are acquainted with the art of the smith; ought we not therefore
to trust souls to him who is well-skilled to soften them by the
fervent heat of the Holy Spirit, and who by the impress of
rational implements may fashion each one of you to be a chosen
and useful vessel? [6]

The great theologian is, of course, pointing up a continuing problem in the Church, that of the worthiness and
competence of the men called to any holy office in the

Church. The problem of the method of choosing bishops is by no means as easy as it seems. Anciently, as in modern times in the American Church, bishops were elected by the acclamation of the clergy and laity of a diocese, with the ensuing ratification of their choice by the other bishops of the province.

In the Byzantine empire and in Europe, the civil rulers as *representative laymen* came, ultimately, to have the exclusive right of nominating bishops—a practice as jealously guarded by Philip II and Louis XIV, as by Elizabeth I and Catherine II—and we must not forget that though this method of choice could produce such non-spiritual men as a du Bois, a Talleyrand, or even that eighteenth-century bishop who, according to Sidney Smith, was an undeniable proof of Apostolic Succession, since the only way to account for him was that he was descended from Judas Iscariot, this procedure could also produce a Fenélon, a Tikhon Zadonsky, and a William Temple.

Neither procedure, however, was that described in the New Testament. However embarrassing, it must be faced that in the New Testament days election, or appointment, was made on the grounds that the Holy Spirit had *already* chosen a man for a specific work. Theologically, this is of vast importance because if this fact is not borne in mind, the whole theory of Order stands a chance of becoming purely mechanical. In this connection, because the Apostles associated bishops and deacons with the public ministry of the Church, two scriptural references must be noted: First, that the *lot*, or *cleros* (from which we ultimately got the word "clergy") which fell upon Matthias was the recognition of a status for which he was *already* qualified.

Second, in the choice of the first deacons, the men were already qualified by the Spirit when the multitude chose them and the Apostles ordained them. Nothing is clearer in the New Testament than the fact that the Apostles in laying their hands on Saul of Tarsas were but confirming an action *already* taken by the Holy Ghost. One must recognize that such procedure assumes an inner life of the Spirit, and a degree of objective judgment on a subjective matter, which few bishops, and not many diocesan conventions, would dare to claim. But difficult as it is, no amount of practical and necessary mechanics must ever be permitted to interfere with that fundamental question in the Ordinal: "Are you persuaded that you are truly called to this Ministry, according to the will of our Lord Jesus Christ, and the order of this Church?" (BCP, p. 541)

The judgment of the Church in this matter of vocation is necessarily almost always pragmatic; but in spite of all of the things which can be said against our system, it is good to remind ourselves of what happens when it really works. Let us consider for a moment the great hero bishop of Milan, St. Ambrose, who was born in about 340. At the age of 34, while governor of Liguria, he made an appearance at the principal church in the interests of inducing peace between two warring factions. After he had finished his address, a little child is reputed to have cried out "Ambrose, Bishop!" Whether this is true or not, he was elected by acclamation, and, even though he was only a catechumen, was ultimately forced to accept the election. He was consecrated bishop less than a week after his baptism. He was a great and courageous man, but there is probably no incident in his life which stands out as dramatically as his refusal to permit the emperor Theodosius, who had just ordered a dreadful massacre, to enter the Portian Church. The emperor stated that he was contrite, but Ambrose insisted that private regrets "were insufficient to expiate so grievous a wrong." The emperor remained under discipline for eight months, and before Ambrose would readmit him to communion, he was forced to issue a law which delayed all capital punishment for thirty days after the date of sentence. This was as much to guard the emperor from the results of his own violent temper as it was to protect the people. In mentioning this famous incident, it is well to bear in mind what Ambrose himself thought about binding and loosing, for this incident was grossly misquoted and misapplied in medieval times to justify the ascendancy of the Church over the State. Ambrose says,

God alone forgiveth sins. The Holy Spirit doth it; and the part which men bear in this action of forgiveness is only applying their Ministry to it, not exercising any direct authority; for they remit sins not in their own, but in the Name of the Father, and of the Son, and of the Holy Ghost. They intercede, but the Deity confers the grant.[7]

Parenthetically, one should note the words ascribed to St. Cyprian—not the most backward of men on the subject of ecclesiastical authority:

Remission of sins, whether by Baptism, or by any other ordinance, is properly, the act of the Spirit of God, and the efficacy of it is to be entirely ascribed to him; whatever agency the Priest may have in it, by words or gestures, or any formularies derived to him from Apostolical institution.[8]

The finest picture of the Church's tenderness, in spite of its sternness, is seen in the form of Absolution which was taking its shape at this period:

O God, our Lord and Governor, who didst present thyself to thy Disciples, when the doors were shut, after having said, 'Peace be unto you. Whosoever sins ye remit, they are remitted unto them; and whosoever sins ye retain, they are retained': Do thou, O Lord God, according to that invisible Almighty power wherewith thou presidest over all things, graciously look upon this thy servant, and by my Ministry, though I am myself a grievous sinner, wash away his guilt, and remove the causes through which he hath contracted it; that he who is bound by the Discipline of the Church, may be loosed from the sin which brought him under it; through thy grace and compassion, O merciful God, whose holy Name, Father, Son and blessed Spirit, be praised and magnified, now and for evermore.[9]

The history of Anglo-Saxon Christianity might have been far happier had Becket been possessed of as gentle and loving a temper.

St. Ambrose's action shows us not only a bishop at his best, but also the whole matter of binding and loosing properly applied. This is the tradition in which we stand, and this is the principle of action to which our bishops are committed. If we are wrong, at least we are wrong in very distinguished company.

From the sixteenth to the twentieth centuries, a vast amount of nonsense was put forward as to the essential form and matter of Ordination. We must recognize that the Greek word used to describe "stretching out the hand" is used exclusively in connection with Ordination. It is not used for any of the other instances of the "laying on of hands" as, for example, in Confirmation, Unction, or the Reconciliation of penitents. Whereas the general, practical virtue of service (*diakonia*) is binding on all Christians, nevertheless, even in New Testament days, the special order of servants, the deacons, were ordained in a special way. They were not *especially* God's servants; rather they were *peculiarly* so. The ancient *matter* of all ordinations was, and still is, the laying on of hands. The ancient *form* of all ordinations was, and still is, prayer.

We know very little about ordination rites existing before the several "Church Orders" which originally date from the commencement of the third century. The words of the prayers have varied markedly. In the consecration of a bishop, in the Apostolic Tradition, we find the following *form:*

Grant, O Father, Reader of the heart, to this thy servant, whom thou hast elected to the episcopate, to feed thy holy flock and to show forth to thee the primacy of the priesthood (*primatum sacerdotii*), serving without blame day and night unceasingly to propitiate thy countenance and to offer the gifts of thy Holy Church, to have, in the spirit of the primacy of the priesthood (*primatus sacerdotii*), power to remit sins according to thy commandment, to give the lots according to thy precept, to loose every bond according to the power which thou didst give to the Apostles, to please thee moreover in meekness and purity of heart, offering thee a sweet-smelling savour: through thy Child (puerum) Jesus Christ, through whom to thee be glory with him and the Holy Spirit. Amen.[10]

The *form* in the Roman Rite, according to its own latest definition, is, surprisingly enough, the following,

Fill up in Thy priest the perfection of Thy ministry and sanctify with the dew of Thy heavenly ointment this Thy servant decked out with the ornaments of all beauty.[11]

In the Eastern Orthodox Church, it is much more difficult to determine the point at which the *form* is applicable. From the Orthodox rubrics, one gathers that the action is cumulative and part of a whole and continuing service.

By the election and approbation of the most God-loving Bishops, and of all the consecrated Council . . .

The grace divine, which always healeth that which is infirm, and completeth that which is wanting, through the laying-on of hands elevateth thee,—duly elected, to be the Bishop of the God-saved city, of. . . .

Wherefore let us pray for him, that the grace of the all-holy Spirit may come upon him.

In the Name of the Father, and of the Son, and of the Holy Spirit, now, and ever, and unto ages of ages.

O Master, Lord our God, who through thine all-laudable Apostle Paul hast established for us an ordinance of degrees and ranks, unto the service and divine celebration of thine august and all-spotless Mysteries upon thy holy Altar; first, Apostles, secondly, Prophets, thirdly, teachers: Do thou, the same Lord of all, who also has graciously enabled this chosen person to come under the yoke of the Gospel and the dignity of a Bishop through the laying-on of hands of us, his fellow Bishops here present, strengthen him by the inspiration and power and grace of thy Holy Spirit, as thou didst strengthen thy holy Apostles and Prophets; as thou didst anoint Kings; as thou hast consecrated Bishops: And make his Bishopric to be blameless; and adorning him with all dignity, present thou him holy, that he may be worthy to ask those things which are for the salvation of the people, and that thou mayest give ear unto him. For blessed is thy Name, and glorified thy Kingdom, of the Father, and of the Son, and of the Holy Spirit, now, and ever, and unto ages and ages. Amen.[12]

In considering our own Ordinal, we must take note of the fact that in modern liturgical terms, the *form*, or prayer, is that which precedes the imposition of hands and the words accompanying it. If one remembers that the phrase "giving to thy family their portion in due season" is the exact New Testament technical language for the work of a bishop, the whole point may be somewhat clearer.

Almighty God, and most merciful Father, who, of thine infinite goodness, hast given thy only and dearly beloved Son Jesus Christ, to be our Redeemer, and the Author of everlasting life; who, after that he had made perfect our redemption by his death, and was ascended into heaven, poured down his gifts abundantly upon men, making some Apostles, some Prophets, some Evangelists, some Pastors and Doctors, to the edifying and making perfect his Church; Grant, we beseech thee, to this thy servant, such grace, that he may evermore be ready to spread abroad thy Gospel, the glad tidings of reconciliation with thee; and use the authority given him, not to destruction, but to salvation; not to hurt, but to help: so that, as a wise and faithful servant, giving to thy family their portion in due season, he may at last be received into everlasting joy; through the same Jesus Christ our Lord, who, with thee and the Holy Ghost, liveth and reigneth, one God, world without end. *Amen.* (BCP, p. 558)

The process by which we have gradually rediscovered the essential *form* and *matter* of ordination has often been both acrimonious and painful. The profound ignorance of ancient formularies, which characterized most churches until recent times, produced a successive set of misconceptions as to what was required. There have been bitter controversies about the necessity of individual intention versus corporate intention, the point at which the intention is announced, the necessity of anointing, the necessity of the tradition (or "handing over") of the instruments, the number of bishops who must always and on every occasion participate in a consecration, and the necessity of certain forms of wording during the laying on of hands, et cetera. Nowadays no one of these is considered important in the total picture.

Through the mercies of God, we have been preserved a church in the fullest meaning of that word. None is more conscious than we that God has not always bound others by the same rules wherewith we are bound—after all, the ultimate power of binding and loosing whether *for* good or *from* sin rests with him. We believe that it is for good that we have been bound to the practice of the ancient Church.

However obscured it has been at times, and however abused by the failings of men, the Apostolic Succession is still the root of all the Christianity you and I know and love and really understand. It was not a one-sided group of churchmen but a broadly representative gathering of clergymen of the Church of England, who in 1922 made this affirmation:

We affirm the essential necessity of the Sacrament of Order according to the institution of Christ, the practice of the Apostles, and the constant tradition of the Church. This is secured in the Churches of the Anglican Communion by the transmission of the several orders of the hierarchy by the imposition of the hands of the bishops, to whom it has been transmitted in like manner by an uninterrupted succession from the days of the Apostles.

We, the undersigned, therefore, hold that our Lord, through the ministry of the successors of the Apostles, has conferred on us and on all the members of the clergy of the Anglican Communion the Sacrament of Order, with the purpose that we, who are priests, should (a) preach and teach the word of God; (b) offer the unbloody sacrifice of the Eucharist both for the living and the departed; (c) sacramentally absolve sinners who repent and confess their sins; and (d) otherwise minister to the flock of Christ according to the ancient faith and practice of the Universal Church.[13]

Let us be perfectly clear, Apostolic Succession is not a theory which will keep us from possible union with other religious bodies; rather, it is a practice which will, in God's own good time, make such a union possible. It is the treasured gift we bring.

IV. ॐ

The Life of Thankfulness

Living
Eucharistically ?~ 12.

To live eucharistically is to live thankfully. To live thankfully is, in part, to live with enthusiasm. The original meaning of the word "enthusiasm" is "in God." People who are "in God," therefore, live in and by the power of God.

People who are Christian are "in God" because they are "in Christ." They can live with enthusiasm because they know Christ in the Eucharist and because they receive him there. They then can live with his power in the world. The God they are "in" and who is "in them" is the God who created and sustains the world, who was in Christ, by whom the world was redeemed in his victory over sin and death on the Cross; who continues to give himself to those he has called under the veil (or signs) of bread and wine in the Eucharist; and who will come again to establish God's kingdom in the world.

Whatever, then, life brings Christian people—burdens or joys, responsibilities or failures, good events or evil, tragedies or victories—those who are "in God" eucharistically can affirm its essential goodness and enter into it with enthusiasm and joy.

This theme can first of all be stated in very direct and simple language. Christians know themselves to be members of a family, the head of which is Jesus Christ. They have been brought into that family through baptism by the action of his Spirit. Whatever the human relationships that surrounded them at the time—parents who "made the arrangements" if they were children, or friends who "influenced" them if they were adults—Christian people recognize that it was the Spirit of God working through those relationships who took the initiative to call them into his family, and make them his children, members of Christ and inheritors of his kingdom.

Once this act had been completed by Confirmation, they were able to share in the Lord's Supper, wherein they remembered the sacrifice of Christ and, by taking spiritually his Body and Blood under the forms of bread and wine, were strengthened and refreshed to live as members of his family. In this act of remembrance they thanked God for all his gifts to them and pre-eminently for the gift of Christ. At the same time they offered themselves to him that they might live as becomes his children.

Thence they go about their business of living, knowing that wherever they go they go "in God," that however difficult life may be, it has been overcome by Christ; that as they live "in him," they too can overcome even the worst power of sin and death. Indeed, they realize that God continues his struggle against these powers through them and that, regardless of all appearances to the contrary, God will prevail. There will be a "coming again" when the (now hidden) power of Christ will be made manifest and all things will be gathered under his dominion and control. Therefore, until that day comes or so long as they live, they will enter upon life with enthusiasm and joy. Come what may, they will be living eucharistically "in God," who was in Christ reconciling the world unto himself, and who now is received in the sacrament of the Eucharist.

The development of this theme depends upon an understanding of four key words. They are: *family, remembrance, thanksgiving,* and *joy.* The purpose of this chapter will be to remind ourselves of what these words mean in their fundamental biblical sense and to interpret their meaning for our eucharistic living today.

To begin with the word *family* is to set forth at the outset the relationship which exists between Christians and God, expressed in the Bible by the word *covenant.* The Old Testament story describes the relationship begun by God wherein he chose Israel to be his people. The history of Israel can be read as the description of how the people responded to his initiative and action. The central biblical emphasis is upon the covenant (or family) relationship established by God. He takes the initiative and then the people respond to him by their worship and by the obedience of their life to his commandments.

This family relationship is made even more intimate in the New Testament where a "new covenant" is established by the life, death, and resurrection of Christ. In

Christ, God did not simply call his people to be his own but he visited and redeemed them. "He loved us and sent his Son to be the propitiation for our sins." (I John 4:10) Christ not only (as God) revealed God to man by descending in love to reconcile man to God, but he also (as man) responded to God in obedience to love and overcame all that separates man from God, in sin and death. The signs of what he has done are in the bread and wine—the cup is the cup of the "new covenant"; Christ himself established this new relationship by his sacrifice. Henceforth the members of his family respond to him in worship through Jesus Christ our Lord, and their living is a grateful response because of what he has already done. Paul describes this by saying that we have been adopted as sons of God (Galatians 4:5)—that relationship which we do not have by nature we are given by God's gracious act in Christ— and henceforth we live *in Christo,* in Christ.

For our purpose the importance of this family relation is threefold. First, our relationship to God in his family is begun by him, not by us. Even on the natural family level the one thing we all have in common is that we are not born nor placed in any particular family by any act of our own. We are here because of a relationship established by our parents, and all we can ever do is to respond to life within that relationship. So with God's relationship to us. It is established by him. Second, since we are members of a family, we know ourselves fully only in relation to other members of our family. We are members of a corporate body; our individuality arises out of common family life. Third, since God has taken the initiative, our worship and our living are always in response to what he has done. God has accomplished certain things for mankind in general and for us in particular and whatever we do then we do in response to him and his action.

To consider what he has done leads us to the next word: *remember*. What do we remember about God and his action? What we remember most, of course, is what he did in Christ: he gave his Son to suffer death upon the Cross for our redemption; Christ "made there (by his one oblation of himself once offered) a full, perfect and sufficient sacrifice, oblation, and satisfaction for the sins of the whole world"; he also commanded us "to continue a perpetual memory of his precious death and sacrifice until his coming again." "This do," he said, "in remembrance of me." (I Cor. 11:24-25; Luke 22:19)

Now the significance of the kind of remembrance of which the Bible speaks is that it is infinitely more than simply "remembering" an historic event. It recalls the past to be sure, but it also brings it into the present so that it continues with power in the present. It is a "re-calling" so that the event of the past continues to affect us now as it once affected others then. It is "the making present" of some event of the past. The Greek word for "recalling"— "to do this in remembrance"—is *anamnesis*. It means to recall before God an event in the past so that it continues to be powerful in the present.

Let us use an analogy. When a man remembers his wedding day he does not simply regard this as an historic event. He can indeed call to mind something of how he felt: the fright, the awe, the mystery, the inability to comprehend why a woman should give herself to him in marriage and the utter sense of thanksgiving that this should be.

So, when we recall "the night in which he was betrayed," we call to mind all that took place in the Upper Room, the breaking of the bread and the blessing of the wine, the signs of the new Covenant between God and his people, and these recall the sacrifice made once and for all on Calvary the following day. We enter into this event now in the present and still it continues to affect and influence us.

The point of the "doing this" is that we might remember *him*. It is *he* who comes into the present with power. It is *his* sacrifice into which we enter which is offered to God. It is *he*—the same yesterday, today and forever—who is present in this eucharistic act. In this sacrament we meet *him*—and this is the reason for our *anamnesis*. We do not, of course, repeat his sacrifice but we do, in this act before the altar of the Church, enter into his continual self-offering before God at the heavenly altar.

The point of a husband remembering his wedding day is not simply to recapture the event. Rather it is to recapture *her* whom he married. As she is remembered (as he celebrates an anniversary for an *anamnesis* of her), she comes with power again into his life; again within the fright and mystery and awe and thankfulness he meets *her*. Furthermore, to her living presence there is added not only all the memories of the "once and for all" giving of her love to him but also all the continued experiences of love, of her self-giving, over the years. He now knows her more profoundly than when he married her.

So to the act of remembrance when we remember "the one oblation of himself once offered," we remember also the continual giving of Christ experienced by us through our lives. He comes to us in the Eucharist, therefore, not only with our memory of what he did "once and for all" but of what he has done for us personally day after day. We thank God "for our creation, preservation, and all the blessings of this life. . . ." Here we take up the Old Testament theme of thanksgiving to God for his acts, not only in establishing the Covenant (e.g., Ex. 12:14; Deut. 16:3), but in nature, "in seedtime and harvest"; and to this theme we add that of the New Testament thanksgiving "above all for thine inestimable love in the redemption of the world by our Lord Jesus Christ, for the means of grace and for the hope of glory." So when we "do this in remembrance," we call to mind all that God has done for us in our individual lives—our families, love given and received, work to do and health enjoyed, whatever our blessings—and especially in his act of sacrifice for all mankind from which our own personal "memories" receive their meaning and continuing power.

Living eucharistically, then, begins for us with our recognition that our worship, as our life, is a response within a family relationship which God has already established for us, and with our act of remembering what he has done once for all mankind in the sacrifice of Christ and for us personally over our lifetime. What *we* do we are enabled to do by him in response to what he has already done and continues to do.

So we come to the third word, *thanksgiving*. The Greek word for thanksgiving is *eucharistia,* whence comes the word *eucharist*. Although in the early Church the word was applied variously to the Christian sacramental prayer, to the whole action or rite of which that prayer furnished the formal verbal expression, and to the elements over which the prayer was uttered, we shall use it in reference to the whole act of the Eucharist itself and thence to the total response of thanksgiving of Christian people in their worship and life to the gift of God in Christ.[1]

Through the service we offer to God "our sacrifice of praise and thanksgiving." This includes the offering of bread and wine and their blessing (or "giving thanks" for them); the prayer of Consecration in which thanks is given to God for his gift of Christ, and the elements are offered in union with his eternal offering; the bread itself is broken; then it is given with the wine to the people as the Body and Blood of Christ spiritually taken and received in communion. "Thus the celebrant does what Christ did, taking bread and wine at the Offertory, blessing them in the great eucharistic prayer, breaking bread at the Fraction, and giving them to the assembled disciples in Communion."[2]

Unworthy though we are, we have in the name of Christ and by virtue of his wholly worthy offering of himself, offered our act of worship, *of praise and thanksgiving,* and received from him his Body and Blood—himself—to live in him, comforted, refreshed, strengthened. We then go about our daily tasks living eucharistically. We have been given Christ under the signs of bread and wine, so our act of worship and our response is one of thanksgiving. "Thus it is," says Olive Wyon,

through him, and through him alone, that we can offer acceptable worship to God at the Eucharist. Here Christ takes our imperfect worship, our stumbling prayers, our weak and fitful
desires as well as our deepest and best longings, and unites them
with his own worship in the heavenly places. Thus through him
we are able to worship the Father in spirit and in truth.[3]

So our final hymn of praise is one in which "we praise
thee, we bless thee, we worship thee, we glorify thee, we
give thanks to thee for thy great glory, O Lord God, heavenly King, God the Father Almighty."

The undergirding and predominant note of the service,
therefore, is one of thanksgiving. We thank God for all
his gifts to us and especially for the gift of Christ. Inevitably this leads to one further step: the spirit of adoration
toward God—not now for anything he does—simply for
what he is: the Creator of the universe who loves us,
from whom we come, before whom we bow down and
worship, upon whom we are dependent, and in whom
we live and move and have our being. All life is in God.
He *is*. Therefore we adore him and cry: "Holy, holy, holy,
Lord God of Hosts. Heaven and earth are full of thy
glory. Glory be to thee, O Lord, most high."

Let us, therefore, expand the word *thanksgiving* to
include *adoration*. We thank God for what he has done
and continues to do; and we bless him because he is. To
live eucharistically is to have this movement of our hearts
toward God permeating everything in our lives.

Eucharistic living, however, if it is to be true to
eucharistic worship, includes yet another form of prayer:
self-offering. The act of thanksgiving includes the total

commitment of ourselves to God that he may dwell in us in our living in the world. To be truly thankful is to praise him "not only with our lips but in our lives." This means the offering of ourselves to him.

As we have seen, part of the eucharistic act is the offering—not simply of bread and wine (elements of the natural order) but as symbols of the offering of ourselves. "Here we offer and present unto thee, O Lord, our selves, our souls and bodies. . . ." It may be of help to think of our offering conjoined with the offering of the bread and wine on the altar, remembering Augustine's description: "There *you* are upon the table; there *you* are in the chalice." Indeed, what we are is not simply our personal selves but more, for we are the Church, the Body of Christ, offered to God.[4] So we offer as part of ourselves, our work, the work of the Church, all that God has created, the world. We are to offer him, in other words, *everything*. This means there is nothing which can be withheld.

Perhaps we can use the words we have been considering as guide posts for our thinking. We offer our prayers and intercessions for the members of a *family*—"for the whole state of Christ's Church." We always bring our concern for the brethren: those whom we know personally and to whom we are bound; those who by position or need have a special claim upon our intercession; those who having died are now members of the family living in closer communion with God. When we go to the altar we do not go alone, but as members of a family and we help bring one another.

Again, we think of our offering in terms of *remembrance*. We offer to God what we remember. The Church has been called a "remembering society." We remember people and the needs of the world. We remember God and his saving act in Christ. We remember the history of the Church and the faithful, especially those who have touched our own lives. In a sense our offering is made up of our memories. What we choose to remember is what we offer.

The danger is obvious. We forget those things we do not want to remember (or, perhaps more accurately, we let them slip into our unconscious where they continue to be borne as burdens). We forget our failures and injustices, but remember the failures and injustices of others. We forget our sins and remember those of our neighbor. We forget our guilt and remember the guilt of others. What we choose to forget and choose to remember determines the quality of the offering of ourselves. Yet this will not do. We cannot offer only our best side and hold back the worst; we can offer only our total selves.

The way by which this can best be done is by taking seriously our third word, *thanksgiving;* and to remember ourselves before God with thanksgiving. This does not mean that we are to thank God for everything we have done. On the contrary, we have done many things which we ought not to have done and have left undone many things which we ought to have done. We can, however, remember them, offer them to God, and then thank him that *he* has forgotten them. He has wiped them away in his forgiveness of us set forth by Christ in his offering. Then—and only then—can we also forget them.

That which separates us from God is our sin. We make only a token offering of ourselves if we forget this, and

pretend that because we try to overlook our sins God has
forgotten them. Yet if we can remember them with thanksgiving to God because we now "have an Advocate with
the Father, Jesus Christ the righteous; and he is in the
Propitiation for our sins." (I John 2:1-2), then their power
is broken, the separation is overcome and we are reconciled
to God by Christ. All this is part of our eucharistic prayer
of thanksgiving. It includes our own self-offering and consecration. We offer ourselves and this means our sinful
selves.

Indeed, this is close to the very heart of the meaning
of the sacrificial offering of Christ. By such an offering of
our sinful selves we acknowledge our own share in the
death of Christ and affirm that it is only as he who knew
no sin takes our sin upon himself can the power of sin
over our lives be broken. This Christ could do only through
his willingness to die for the love of God. The resurrection
and the power that came from it is the evidence that God
destroyed both the power of sin and the power of death.
And it is this victory which is now ours and which we
share as we truly offer ourselves to him.

There is one further word about this prayer of thanksgiving. True thanksgiving, as we have seen, incorporates
the total offering of the Body of Christ; it means the
thankful presentation to God of our sins; and it includes,
finally, the offering of our *suffering* to him. And again the
key is to offer our sufferings with thanksgiving.

There is here a great mystery. We can be neither glib
nor sentimental about suffering; we cannot easily speak
of its value, nor can we pretend that it is either human
or right to enjoy it. Yet if we can realize how it is woven
into the very structure of life and how it is embedded in

the innermost meaning of the Cross, then we can come to understand how as we enter into the sacrifice of Christ in the Eucharist we are enabled to share in his atoning life—*then* we can be thankful.

Nobody likes suffering. Suffering is an evil, part of existence in a world "fallen" from God. Christ did not like suffering. Nowhere in the Gospels did he act as though suffering in itself was good. Indeed, in that climactic experience in the Garden of Gethsemane on the night in which he was betrayed, he asked God to take his cup of suffering away. Yet it was not taken away. It remained. It had to be faced. And *he* could not turn away. It was there and if he was to do God's will he had no alternative but to take it. So he took it—*for the love of God*—and he offered it back to him that his will might be done.

Clearly God's will could be done there only as he took the suffering and offered it to him. And this is the mystery: God's will is done precisely through suffering. It was as Christ took it for his love of his Father knowing that this meant his death on the Cross that God was then able to raise him from the dead victorious over sin and death and all the powers that made suffering rampant in the world. Then there was set loose in the world the Spirit of God to wage battle against those forces of evil. The Holy Spirit was poured out upon the faithful company of men who continued in faith in Christ; and in the history of the Church the work of the Holy Spirit begins. So this Spirit continues to do battle against the demonic powers of darkness to this day. The atoning work of Christ which assured God's victory over the forces of evil was accomplished only because he accepted suffering and offered it to God as part of his sacrifice of love for him and for the world.

But the battle continues. Though by Christ's victory we are assured of the ultimate victory, we still live in a world where the power of sin and death have not yet spent themselves. So we too face suffering. When it is not taken away and we cannot in conscience avoid it, then we are given an opportunity to share in the atoning work of Christ. Then as we accept our suffering for the love of God and offer it back to him, we make it possible for his Spirit to go ahead just so much further in the world.

Indeed, as for Christ, so for us: God's will finally can be done only as we accept suffering and offer it to him as part of our sacrifice. Because we have been given the opportunity to serve him in this way, because we know it is the best way, because it is God's way, and because we are here brought most intimately into union with Christ's own sacrifice, this is an offering we can make *with thanksgiving*. This is the secret of eucharistic living on its deepest and most profound level.

Therefore, we shall take our sufferings in this life— our sorrows, failures, responsibilities, griefs, and bereavements, whatever they may be—and offer them to God, together with the offering of Christ in the Eucharist. We can be confident that in some mysterious hidden way this is how we are called to take our part in Christ's continuing redemption of the world—and we shall be thankful.

We come naturally then to our final word, *joy*. Do you remember Baron Von Hügel's estimate of joy? "The divinely intended end of our life," he writes,

is joy overflowing and infinite . . . There is a wholesome, a strengthening *zest* attached to all action which is right and appropriate for the agent . . . Now there is no zest comparable to the zest, expansion, the joy brought to the soul by God and the soul's close union with Him . . . The general direction . . . [is] . . . the love of God above all things and the love of our neighbor as ourselves. And this love of God, where uninhibited and full, brings Joy—it seeks God, Joy; and it finds Joy, God.[5]

The assurance that this is so is found in the Eucharist. The action of the Eucharist is not only a looking backward; it is also a looking forward. There is not only the *anamnesis,* by which the past action of Christ is brought forward into the present; there is also the anticipation by which the future action of Christ is brought back into the present. We receive in the Eucharist Christ who was and who is and who is also yet to come. The pledges we take are of him who shall come again. In this act we are with Christ in the night in which he was betrayed, in his death, in his resurrection, with him in the bread and wine, and with him in his coming again. His work shall be completed when he comes to establish his kingdom, so we participate not only in the Last Supper but also in the Messianic Banquet.

So there is always this final note of "eschatological joy." This is the joy derived from the "last things" under the control of the same Christ whom we remember and whom we receive now in the Eucharist.

The biblical description puts it this way. The world which God created and redeemed will be restored in Christ at the end of time. His rule, now partial in the lives of believers, will become complete in all men and the act of redemption will be fulfilled among the nations and in the world of nature. All the partial victories of God's Spirit will be made whole, and the entire creation will give praise to

him. All that we do as our share in his life will be fulfilled
and we shall take our rightful places in the glory of the
redemption of the whole creation. Then shall there be that
perfect order and harmony when all of God's creation shall
cry,

Holy, holy, holy is the Lord God, the Almighty who was and
who is and who is to come . . . Worthy art thou, our Lord and
our God, to receive the glory and the honor and power, for thou
didst create all things, and by thy will they existed and were
created. (Revelation 4:8-11 RSV)

The future, in other words, is Christ's. Since we are his
we can enter upon that future with joy. Nothing can make
us afraid, nothing can finally harm us, nothing—not even
death—can ever separate us from him. We can go about
the business of living, not cast down because of temporary
defeats, not drawing back from the evils that may befall us,
unafraid of anything except of disloyalty to him. So long
as we remain "in him," we will share in his victory over all
the powers set against him. Life is meant to be lived and
we shall embark upon it "with the love of God above all
things and the love of our neighbor as ourselves." This is
the life of joy, and it is ours.

Perhaps the highest that can be said of our living eucharistically, is that we are meant to be bearers of joy as
we step into the future of tomorrow. "The divinely intended
end of our life is joy overflowing and infinite." Until that
end come we can enter upon all the experiences of life "in
God." Since that God is the Christ who is known by us in
the Eucharist, our living "in him" will be living in joy. That
is the end of our Christian living—tomorrow. And the first
step into tomorrow is today.

Notes 🐦

1. HOLY BAPTISM

1. Alec R. Vidler, *Witness to the Light* (New York: Scribner's, 1948), p. 62. Used with permission.
2. *Ibid.*
3. *Ibid.*, p. 63.
4. John Henry Newman, *The Dream of Gerontius.*
5. F. W. Dillistone, *Christianity and Symbolism* (Philadelphia: Westminster, 1955), p. 186. Used with permission.
6. Isaiah 51:9, 10 (quoted in Dillistone, *op. cit.*, p. 190).
7. Dillistone, *op. cit.*, p. 191.
8. *Ibid.*, p. 192

2. PREPARING FOR THE SACRAMENTAL LIFE

1. Copyright 1942, by Stephen Vincent Benet. Inquiries regarding it to be addressed to Brandt and Brandt, 101 Park Avenue, New York, N.Y. Used by permission.
2. Friedrich Von Hügel, *The Mystical Element of Religion,* Vol. I, p. 241.
3. Alan Paton, "Meditation, For a Young Boy Confirmed," *The Christian Century* LXXI, 41 (Oct. 13, 1954), 1237-39. By permission of the author and of The Christian Century Foundation.
4. London: Collins, 1953.
5. Angela Morgan. Quoted by Olive Wyon in *The School of Prayer* (Napierville, Ill.: Allenson, 1958). Used with permission.

3. CONFIRMATION

1. Attributed to Archbishop Laud.
2. John Cosin, "Confirmation" in *Anglicanism,* ed. by P. E. Moore and F. L. Cross (London: S.P.C.K., 1951), p. 444.
3. Quoted in *Liturgy and Worship,* ed. by W. K. Lowther Clarke and C. Harris (London: S.P.C.K., 1954), p. 457. Used with permission.
4. W. K. Lowther Clarke, quoting E. G. Howe, in *Liturgy and Worship,* p. 456.
5. Report of the Diocesan Commission on Preparation for Confirmation. The Diocese of New York, *Journal of the One Hundred and Seventy-Eighth Convention of the Diocese of New York* (New York: Synod Hall, 1959), p. 156. Used with permission.

4. THE HEAVENLY BANQUET

1. See L. Ginzberg, *Legends of the Jews* (Philadelphia: Jewish Publication Society of America), I, 27-29.
2. See my essay in F. E. Johnson, ed., *Religious Symbolism* (New York: Harper, 1955), pp. 5-8.

7. THE COMMUNION

1. Didache, or Teaching of the Apostles, in *Documents of the Christian Church,* ed. by Henry Bettenson (New York and London: Oxford University Press, 1947). Used with permission.

8. THE ASSURING HAND: ABSOLUTION

1. *The First and Second Prayer Books of Edward VI* (New York: Dutton, Everymans Library), p. 217.
2. See Luke 15:11-24.

9. THE HEALING HAND: UNCTION

1. The Standing Liturgical Commission of the Protestant Episcopal Church in the United States of America, *Prayer Book Studies*, III, The Order for the Ministration to the Sick (New York: The Church Pension Fund, 1951), p. 4.
2. This paragraph and substantial sections of the presentation which follows were originally set forth in the author's book, *The Ministry of Healing* (New York: Morehouse-Barlow, © 1959), pp. 20-24; 28; 38-39; 76-77; and 91f. Used with the permission of Morehouse-Barlow.
3. Simon Doniger, ed., *Healing: Human and Divine* (New York: Association Press, 1957). Used with permission.
4. Alexis Carrel, *Voyage to Lourdes* (London: Harper & Bros., 1950), pp. 38-39; 23-24; 91f. Used with permission.
5. *Liturgy and Worship*, ed. by W. K. Lowther Clarke and Charles Harris (London: S.P.C.K., 1954), p. 628. Used with permission.

10. JOINING HANDS: HOLY MATRIMONY

1. For a short account see Massey H. Shepherd, *The Oxford American Prayer Book Commentary* (New York: Oxford University Press, 1950), p. 300f.

2. Emil Brunner, *The Divine Imperative* (Philadelphia: Westminster Press, 1947). Used with permission.

11. *APOSTOLIC HANDS: HOLY ORDER*

1. Walter Kelly Firminger, "The Ordinal," in *Liturgy and Worship,* ed. by W. K. Lowther Clarke and Charles Harris (London: S.P.C.K., 1954), p. 628. Used with permission.
2. John Knox, *Early Church and the Coming Great Church* (New York: Abingdon, 1955), p. 110. Used with permission.
3. Henry Charles Lea, *A History of the Inquisition of Spain* (New York: Macmillan, 1906).
4. Firminger, "The Ordinal," in *Liturgy and Worship,* p. 642.
5. Tertullian on Tradition and Succession. *De praescriptione haereticorum,* xxxii, in *Documents of the Christian Church,* ed. by Henry Bettenson (London: Oxford University Press, 1943), p. 100. Used with permission.
6. Philip Schaff and Henry Wace, ed., *A Select Library of Nicene and Post Nicene Fathers of The Christian Church* (New York: The Christian Literature Company, 1893), p. 537.
7. Nathaniel Marshall, *The Penitential Discipline of the Primitive Church, For the First Four Hundred Years After Christ; Together with Its Declension from the Fifth Century, Downwards to Its Present State: Impartially Represented* (Oxford: John Henry Parker, 1844), p. 71.
8. *Ibid.*
9. *Ibid.,* p. 209.
10. Firminger, "The Ordinal," in *Liturgy and Worship,* p. 630.
11. "Ceremony of Consecration of His Excellency the Most Reverend John Joseph Maguire, D.D., Titular Bishop of Antiphrae, Auxiliary Bishop to the Archbishop of New York" (New York: Cathedral of St. Patrick, 1959), p. 17.

12. Isabel Florence Hapgood, *Service Book of the Holy Orthodox-Catholic Apostolic Church* (New York: Association Press, 1922), p. 329. Used with permission.

13. Mgr. Chrysostom Papadopoulos, *The Validity of Anglican Ordinations;* trans. by J. A. Douglas (London: The Faith Press, 1931), p. 68. Used with permission.

12. *LIVING EUCHARISTICALLY*

1. Dom Gregory Dix, *The Shape of the Liturgy* (Westminster: Dacre Press, 1949).

2. W. Nicholls, *Jacob's Ladder* (London: Lutterworth Press, 1958).

3. Olive Wyon, *The Altar Fire* (Philadelphia: Westminster Press, 1954).

4. A. G. Hebert, ed., *The Parish Communion* (London: S.P.C.K., 1937).

5. Friedrich Von Hügel, *The Life of Prayer* (New York: Dutton, 1927). Used with permission.